LIVE LIKE YOU MEAN IT

On the R.O.A.D. of Life,
There Are Those Who Ride
and Those Who Drive ...
Make Your Choice!

By Ken Wasco and
Ellyn Luros-Elson

Helm Publishing

Copyediting: Dollie Parsons
Cover design: Alain Pendon, Computrition, Inc.
Layout: Pat Dodge, Pages Communications Service

Printed in the United States of America

Helm Publishing
213 Main Street/ P.O. Box 2105
Lake Dallas, TX 75065
940-497-3558 phone
940-497-2927 fax

Orders: 877-560-6025
www.helmpublishing.com

ISBN 0-9787829-0-9

Dedication

To the thousands of wonderful men and women who
inspired us to write this book and to the hundreds
of thousands of individuals we've yet to meet—may
this book empower all of you to start your engines
and live like you mean it.

Acknowledgements

My first thank you goes to the first person of my life. This work found its beginning in the belief my wife, Jan, has always had in God's plan for me. She helps me see beyond what I am to what I can be. I love you, Jan, and thank you for sharing your life with me. I especially thank our daughters, Shannon, my personal editor, who taught me the value of fewer words, and Lauren, who continues to remind me to "just breathe" as I handle the challenges of an all too busy life. You three are my world, and I can't express strongly enough how important you are to me.

I also thank Paul, John, Dan, John Jr. and Jim Gordon, as well as all my co-workers at Gordon Food Service. You have helped me find my voice and are a constant inspiration. Thank you to my friends at all the "acronym organizations" for listening to my tired jokes and repetitious stories while providing me a forum to continually hone my speaking skills. I am grateful to friends Joyce Hagen-Flint, Bill St. John and Sandy Wagner, who never cease to encourage me. And finally, many thanks to our skillful editor, Jane Grant Tougas, and to my awesomest of friends, Ellyn Luros-Elson, and her fantastic family. Ellyn, will you ever forget that moment backstage at Disneyland when I looked at you and said, "We should write a book!" It's been fun—and it's only beginning.

—Ken Wasco

~~~~~

I want to thank my parents, Ruth and Sam Green, for always encouraging me to be the best that I could be, and my children, Hilary, Jodi, Jason and Stephanie, for their love and support no matter how much I worked or what I wanted to try. They never complained (not much, anyway!) when I missed things that were important in their lives due to my travel schedule.

I want to thank my dear friend, Vicki Briskman, who is always honest with me, even when she knows I don't want to hear what she is saying. Thank you to my great friend, confidant and husband, Lawrence M. Elson, whose wonderful love for life, and for me, inspires me to keep up the race. To my dear friend and colleague Ken and his wife, Jan, and their children, thanks for hanging in there to get this project to completion. And last but not least, a million thanks to our talented editor, Jane Grant Tougas, for the hundreds of hours we shared completing this book.

—Ellyn Luros-Elson

Introduction

On the R.O.A.D. with Ken and Ellyn

A Conversation

Ken: Well, Ellyn, can you believe that it's been 7 years since we first hit the R.O.A.D. on our journey writing this book? I remember hearing you give a presentation in Grand Rapids, and I knew then and there that you were the one I wanted to work with. Some might say we're an odd pair—a nice Southern girl from Los Angeles and a good Polish boy from Grand Rapids—but we shared a common dream. And we really practiced what we preach to get this book into the hands of readers.

Ellyn: It took us a while, but that's okay. We learned a lot along the way. I feel even more strongly today that people need to have dreams in their lives, and they need plans to make those dreams come true. I am amazed that people will take months, maybe even a year or more, to plan a 2-week vacation, but won't spend even 2 weeks thinking about where they want to go in life and making a plan to get there.

Ken: We can stand at the curb and watch life speed by or jump in the car and take the trip of a life time. We can just go along for the ride or get behind the wheel and drive. The choice is ours. That's living like you mean it. The more you and I thought about how so many people travel through life without any direction, the more we felt the need for step-by-step directions to help people move from where they are now to where they want to be, and beyond. And here it is: Look ahead and follow the R.O.A.D.: **R**ecognize your dream. **O**ptimize your situation. **A**ct on your vision. **D**eliver the results.

Ellyn: We've gathered our thoughts and experiences in this book and organized them into a process that can help readers identify a dream and set goals, make the changes necessary to pursue those goals, and do what it takes to achieve their dream. As people read the book and go through the process, I think they will learn firsthand that when they are committed to making their own life meaningful, they can't help but have a positive impact on others along the way. As our readers travel this R.O.A.D., we hope they achieve four important insights:

- Each person controls his or her choices and attitudes.
- There are no failures or mistakes, only lessons learned and wisdom gained.
- The journey to a goal may turn out to be more meaningful than the goal itself.
- Helping others achieve their goals can be the most rewarding journey of all.

Ken: We've laid out this R.O.A.D. map in four sections, each having three chapters. Throughout the book, we've included Travel Log Tips—stories or comments about our own experiences. And at the end of each chapter, we've included some Travel Planning questions and exercises to help our readers think about their own situation. They can take the time to think about the questions and answer them as they read the book, or they can simply look the questions over and answer them later. We've also sprinkled the text with some icons that are designed to call special attention to an idea.

GO	Go for It!	**REST STOP**	Pause and Consider.
	There's No Turning Back.	**STOP**	Stop!
CAUTION	Be Careful!	**U TURN**	Turn It Around.
	Bright Idea!		

Ellyn: It's time we turn it over to our readers, Ken.

Ken: We wish them all a great trip as they make the choice to: Live like you mean it.

Table of Contents

Section 1: Recognize

Section 2: Optimize

Section 3: Act

Section 4: Deliver

R = RECOGNIZE

R
O
A
D

Section 1

"Our truest life is when we are in dreams awake."
—Henry David Thoreau, author

Go for It!

 There's No Turning Back.

 Be Careful!

 Bright Idea!

 Pause and Consider.

 Stop!

 Turn It Around.

1

Wheel Spinning
Caught Up in Keeping Up

Often, lives are defined by a moment in time—an experience that separates everything that came before from all that will follow. Alex can take you back to the exact day that it happened for him, a moment he will never forget.

It began at a party Alex's wife, Liz, planned for her mother who was turning 50. Liz had invited everyone from her side of the family to join in the celebration. Grandparents, aunts and uncles, a few young cousins, Liz's siblings and her father arrived together in what seemed like one giant caravan. Alex had married Liz a little more then a year before. He had since grown quite familiar with family events. After each gathering, Liz would turn to him and ask, "Al, how did you do this time?"

And Alex would respond by saying, "Well, they're a crazy bunch—that's for sure—but they're growing on me."

Today, Alex sits holding his breath in anticipation of what will happen next. Everyone is in the family room when Liz's Uncle Steve breaks the silence.

"All right, now," he says, "it's May 7, my sister Deb's birthday. I think we should go around the room and have everybody try to remember what they were doing on May 7, 20 years ago."

The stories and the laughter continue as each person takes a turn. When it comes back to Steve, he says, "Liz and Alex, you don't get to play because 20 years ago, Liz was only 3. And Alex, you weren't much older." He volunteers, "20 years ago, I was the big man on the high school campus—star athlete, valedictorian, babe magnet."

"Babe magnet? Valedictorian? Star athlete? Is that what he's been telling you, Joan?" Deb asks her sister-in-law. "This guy spent the football season on the bench because his grades were so bad the coach wouldn't let him play. And as I recall, Steve, you spent your senior prom night playing poker with the boys in the basement."

"Don't believe a word of it, Joanie. My sister is losing her mind in her old age," Steve says.

"Doubtful. I think you just spent too much time on Fantasy Island," Joan replies.

"Twenty years ago was a special time for us," Liz's father, Rich, chimes in. "Do you remember what happened the year we turned 30, Deb?"

Their eyes meet as they touch hands. "How could I forget?" she answers. "That was when everything changed for the better. I'll always consider that year our turning point. We had to go through everything we did so that we could be where we are today. I don't think I quite understood that back then, but you did, Rich, and I believed in you." She leans to give her husband a kiss, which is accompanied by a chorus of collective sighs from the guests. Then Liz yells from the kitchen, "Cake time!" and the living room empties as people head out to the porch.

Alex grabs his father-in-law, Rich, by the arm as they pick up the drink glasses. "Mr. Johnson, Dad, could I ask you something?" he says.

Sensing that the question was important, the older man sits back down. "Sure, Alex, what would you like to know?" he responds.

"Well, sir, I've been around all of you for a while now, and to tell you the truth, I've always wondered what happened to you in your life that brought about all the happiness in this house," Alex explains.

"Well, Alex," Rich replies, "it's a long story. Someday, I'll give you the full version, but for brevity's sake, I'll summarize it now. The reason 20 years ago was such an important time in our lives is that it was the year that followed the two before it. Those were the 'dark years,' and we thought the bottom had dropped out. Deb was home with three kids, we had bills we couldn't afford and we were on a treadmill living one day to the next. Then I was called into my boss's office and placed on a permanent lay-off."

"Gosh, Dad," Alex exclaims, "I never knew. So what you are telling me is that all of that tragedy inspired you to get another job and try even harder?"

The older man leans forward for emphasis. "No, Alex, that's not what I am saying at all," Rich counsels. "What you call a 'tragedy' was actually the best thing that could have ever happened to Deb and me. We were living in the fast lane, but we weren't going anywhere. Keeping up with the Joneses was hard work and, frankly, not all it's cracked up to be. There were signs all around us, but we never paid attention to them."

"Signs?" Alex asks.

"Warning signs," Rich explains, "to let us know we were burning the candle at both ends. I was in a state of constant frustration, having headaches, getting into arguments and having trouble sleeping. Something had to break and boy, did it ever."

"Your job?" Alex says.

"Right," says Rich, "but that was a good thing. You see, it wasn't until that job ended that Deb and I had the time to make some new decisions. It was then that I discovered that I didn't need to depend on someone else to be happy. I needed to depend on myself. I consider myself to be one of the lucky ones. I was given a break—a break in the action—a chance to retune my engine, get a new roadmap and start again. Only this time, I was going to take in the scenery and enjoy the companionship along the way."

"Yeah, but you didn't have a job," Alex protests. "Weren't you worried that you weren't going to make it?"

"Why?" Rich asks. "Because I had failed? Failure can be a good thing. In fact, it's a great thing if you learn from it."

"What did you learn?" Alex inquires.

Rich replies, "If you're asking for a short cut to fulfillment in life, you won't get that from me, Alex. Let me tell you something a very smart person once told me. He said that the past was where it belonged and to leave it there, that our eyes and feet are pointed forward for the same reason—to get us where we need to go. And then," Rich continues, "my smart friend repeated something I had heard him say many times before: 'All we are given is this moment and the chance to make the best of it.' For some reason, on that day, I finally heard and understood him."

"The choice to change or move forward is always yours to make?" asks Alex.

"Exactly!" Rich replies. "My father-in-law gave me that bit of advice the first time we sat and had a serious talk. And now I am giving it to you. Success in life is all about that simple idea: All we are given is this moment and the chance to make the best of it. And you know what?" Rich exclaims. "Now is the moment for me to get a piece of cake!"

~~~~~~

Although people differ from each other in many ways, we do share some fundamental traits, such as how we use information. Sometimes we use information for entertainment; sometimes we use it for learning. And we've never had more options for both. The Internet, radio and television, along with countless other media, bombard us with endless choices.

Regardless of whether we are seeking amusement or personal growth—or both—information gives the fuel we need to dream. At one time or another in life's journey, each of us has unique, personal and very specific dreams. How often do you find yourself thinking, "If only I could _____ (you fill in the blank) buy that dream car, get into the right school, get the job I want, get a promotion, find my soul mate, be happy"—the list goes on and on.

TRAVEL LOG TIP:
Some people learned early on that to make things happen they had to do it for themselves. Others learn this lesson a little later in life. The joy of youth is the belief in possibilities and the ability to pursue them. Youth isn't so much chronological as it is attitudinal. *Ken*

NOTES:

Whether it's a fantasy or a quest, most people dream about being better off tomorrow than they are today. Of course, the definition of "better off" is unique to each person. To some, it's having more money; to others, it's being more involved in society and in making the most of their lives; and to still others, it's simply having a closer relationship with their spouse, friends or even God.

Basically, we're always looking, exploring and trying things on for size. If what we find works, we keep it. If it works only for a little while, we start over. We do this constantly because our human nature desires to experience more, and for some people, that means actively seeking personal growth.

Road Trip!

When we learn, experience or gain some new knowledge or insight, we take a step on the road toward self-actualization—that is, successfully developing and using our personal talents. Knowing that this outcome is waiting just around the corner is a big motivator all by itself. At our core, each of us secretly craves personal accomplishment; success is a desire that all humans share. How does it feel when you land a new job, make the sale or get your ideas across? The need to feel accomplishment is programmed into our nature.

Infants learn almost immediately that positive actions result in positive responses. When a baby first smiles, rolls over, sits up, stands up, talks and walks, parents gush with praise. As we grow, we constantly strive to take our game to the next level, knowing that our actions will bring about more praise.

> TRAVEL LOG TIP:
> Someone I worked with once told me about the three people inside of everyone: the person who does what he is supposed to do for his career; the person who works for his family and the people around him he loves; and the person he would be if he were free of all responsibility—the person we dream about being. My friend's counsel to me was that I would find fulfillment by putting that third person to work with the other two.   *Ken*
>
> NOTES:

At the beginning of life, our caregivers give us constant affirmation and reinforcement for everything we do. As we mature, we move from wanting and needing total dependence on those who care for us to a moment when we both want and need to be *independent*. Unfortunately, we may not always have someone there to cheer us on. Healthy people learn to compensate for this by giving positive reinforcement to themselves, thus continuing to grow. Others need to wait for or seek out approval before they can find the strength to act.

No matter what the source of affirmative energy, that feeling of a job well done or a situation well handled is gas in our tank. It provides the fuel to move forward. Whether it's externally given or internally created, affirmation creates an on-ramp to the next challenge. Each trial and each accomplishment brings a feeling of growth. *Bring it on! We can do more—we can do it all! Let's go!*

Naturally, one affirmation leads to the desire for more. Praise motivates us to keep moving toward the next "thing" that worked as well as the last "thing" did. Somewhere along the line, however, people stop passing out rewards for free. Eventually, the praise comes because you stay in your lane—in other words, you follow the rules. It's not so much *what* you do that counts, but rather that you do it the way others expect you to—and don't ask questions.

Gotta This, Gotta That

Now the road toward growth is a bit more complicated. It involves more than just encouragement. The people in our lives begin expecting things of us, and what they want inevitably has an impact on us. We're expected to get with the program and to keep up. Influences such as school, sports and peer groups create an environment in which we are no longer on a level playing field; rather, we are placed in direct competition for success. It is here that we find ourselves forced to either follow the crowd to keep up the pace or simply get left behind. The race of our lives has begun.

> TRAVEL LOG TIP:
> Do you feel like the world is getting smaller and time is moving faster than ever before? In reality, the world is the same size it's always been and time is moving at the same rate it always has. What has changed for all of us is the pace of life.   *Ken*
>
> NOTES:

Our needs, their needs—they all blur together in confusing "activity traps." Too many people want too much from us. Harder, faster, longer becomes a way of life focused only on the here and now. Wanting to do something gives way to having to do it. These wheel-spinning activities are what author Robert Kriegel refers to in *If It Ain't Broke, Break It,* as the "gottas"—the things you just gotta do to keep up.[1] Invariably, they involve pleasing others or serving others' perceptions of you. *When you place these needs ahead of your own, you end up in the "gotta" rut.*

Look around! The signs that life is too fast paced are everywhere. With computers, email, cell phones and pagers, we've made ourselves accessible to everyone 24/7. The business of providing trade-offs and short-cuts is thriving. People will do whatever it takes to maintain their image and stay in the race—personally and professionally. Workshops and seminars offer quick skills without in-depth understanding; "reading" abridged books on tape saves time; mail-order degrees offer instant credibility. The biggest house, the biggest mortgage and as many credit cards as you can get are the price of keeping up with those around you.

> TRAVEL LOG TIP:
> A lot of people use every excuse in the book to justify why they get into financial trouble. One sure way is to spend money you don't have. It's as simple as that! Yes, there are catastrophic events such as illness, but most bankruptcies today are from credit card debt and simple overspending—in other words, not being in control of your life choices.[2] *Ellyn*
>
> NOTES:

Isn't it ironic that in these fast times, the most popular spectator sport is NASCAR? Is it not a metaphor for our lives? The sport involves finely tuned, technologically advanced smart machines that are placed in a confined space where the whole point is to run around the track faster than everybody else. And next year, they'll have to run even faster.

Our lives have become like a NASCAR race; there is a beginning, a middle and an end to our daily run. The biggest difference lies in the fact that NASCAR is just a race. At the end, someone walks away the winner. But if we let life speed by as fast as cars on a racetrack, we risk losing everything along the way. Thanks to consequences like stress, physical ailments, depression, and divorce, a fast-paced lifestyle often produces more losers than winners.

When all that matters is keeping up with those around you, opportunities for a quick fix look like viable options. But in reality, they are nothing more than duct tape on a radiator hose. The problem may be solved—but only for the short-term. For example, finance people love to use the word "leverage" to soften the implications of increased borrowing. Grab any newspaper and you'll be faced with a series of enticing offers like "90 days same as cash" and "no payments 'til March of next year." These are tempting disguises that allow you to have now and pay later. Borrowing from the future may get you what you want now, but it can also create serious roadblocks for you later. Eventually, someone has to pay, and more often than not that someone is you.

> **TRAVEL LOG TIP:**
> The reason dreams stay only dreams for some of us is that we don't take that one extra step. We accept mediocrity, doing just enough to get by—just enough to graduate, just enough to keep our job. When we look at people who have "made it," we say they were lucky. Sure, luck may have something to do with it, but the bottom line is that those who make it have passion for what they do. They go the extra mile. Move your life forward. Act on your dreams.   *Ellyn*
>
> **NOTES:**

The Rearview Mirror

It can be just as dangerous to dwell in the past as it is to get caught up in the present. For every forward-motivated person, there seems to be a hundred who want to stop the clock—or even better, turn back the hands to the "glory days" or to a simpler time. Golden oldies are all the rage, and not just in music. Vintage clothing, furniture and even appliances get top dollar. That's right, even avocado green and harvest gold appliances are selling at a premium to people who yearn for the "way life used to be."

For many, the past represents a time when options seemed more open and possibilities endless. Memories and nostalgia are fine in moderation because they instill an appreciation for history and put the present in perspective. Clinging to the past, however, inhibits growth. We become stagnant, unable to move forward. Most often this happens when people are insecure or fearful of what they will find on the road ahead. Life is a forward action, an evolution. There's no going back. No relationship stays the same. No job stays the same. No person stays the same. Life is about looking ahead and moving forward to get where you want to go. Learn from your past choices and decisions. *You have the control, so take it. There's no going back.*

TRAVEL PLANNING
Where are you going?

As a teenager, what did you want to be? _____

Why was becoming that so important at the time? _____

_____

If you didn't do it, why not? _____

What is your number one dream today? _____

_____

Describe how achieving that dream would make you feel? _____

_____

Everyone has some successes. List some of yours.

    ____ High school graduate   _____ Good parent

    ____ College graduate   _____ Good friend

    ____ Successful relationship   _____ Good job

    ____ Good employer/boss

    ____ Others: _____

Which of these are you most proud of? _____

_____

What has been your most challenging accomplishment so far? _____

_____

_____

Finish this sentence:

    Things would be wonderful, if only I could_____

_____

Finish this sentence:

    I'd be better off today if only I had _____

_____

Are there obstacles in your path?

Describe the "you" who you want to be. _____

_____

_____

_____

_____

_____

Describe some of the work you will have to do to get there. _____

_____

_____

_____

_____

_____

Check off all that apply to you. I need to be the:

_____ Perfect spouse   _____ Perfect boss

_____ Perfect parent   _____ Perfect employee

_____ Perfect brother or sister   _____ Perfect volunteer

_____ Perfect partner in a relationship   _____ Perfect host

_____ Perfect friend   _____ Perfect guest

_____ Perfect (you name it) _____

Now answer this question:

I need to be perfect

_____ For myself? _____ For someone else's approval?

Do you have the resources you'll need for your journey?

Do you have anything in your possession that you wish you had never purchased? _____

_____

_____

_____

_____

_____

List three things you own that you'd like to have the money back for right now.

_____

_____

_____

_____

_____

_____

_____

List three ways you are overspending your energy, time and promises.

_____

_____

_____

_____

_____

_____

2

Getting in Gear

From This Moment On

Carole's position in her company is unique. Having been with the organization for many years, she has become a corporate ambassador. It's a job that few of her colleagues fully understand, but all admire. Most of them know when the time is right to get Carole involved: If the situation requires an industry expert, an eloquent spokesperson, or someone who is widely networked, Carole gets the call.

In the corporate world, however, where jockeying for position is the norm and strength is signaled by office location or the number of people who work for you, Carole holds little "position power." Her office is around a corner and down a long hallway. But Carole doesn't need to be "visible" because when she is in the office, people at every level seek her out. In other words, Carole has what business textbooks refer to as "informal power."

Sue, a new employee, has heard about Carole and wants to get to know her better. Her admiration for Carole started at the orientation for new hires, where Sue listened as the company president described the organizational chart. When he got to Carole's role, he smiled and described her as someone every organization needed. "It's Carole who can look at the A, B and C of a situation," he said, "and correctly identify that somewhere in the future G will happen." The organization had recognized Carole's talent early on and had allowed her to develop—to everyone's benefit.

Later, Sue listened carefully as Carole closed the orientation session. Speaking from her heart and inspiring each person to keep his or her gaze focused forward, Carole's dynamic closing words were, "Believe in yourself. Believe in your ideas. Find someone to share them with—someone who will listen. And remember, you can always call on me." That's when Sue knew for sure she wanted to get to know Carole.

Now, Sue is curious if a situation like Carole's could develop for her within the company. One evening, she sees that Carole's office light is on and decides if there was ever a "right time" to talk with Carol, this would be it. Standing 20 feet down the hall, Sue listens to Carole's laughter as she concludes a phone conversation. After a minute or so of silence, Sue makes her move.

"Hi, Carole," Sue says brightly. "Working late tonight?"

"Oh, hi, Sue," Carole replies. "Yeah, just wrapping some things up before I hit the road again. How about you? What are you still doing here?"

"Well, in all honesty," Sue confesses, "I was hoping to get a chance to talk with you. I realize it's after 6 p.m. now, but do you have a few minutes?"

"Oh, my gosh, yes! Absolutely, come on in," Carole says warmly. "Let me move a couple of these piles around so we have some space on the desk. Sorry it's kind of messy. I just do the 'pile management' thing. I never quite get to the bottom of the pile, but I do keep moving it around! Let me grab a notepad."

"You won't need to write anything down," Sue assures her. "It's more personal—professional, but personal. Since I started to work here, I have been observing you. Everybody loves you here, and you have the neatest job. You do a lot of speaking for the company and get involved in sales presentations. I hear you are on a couple boards, too. What is your job, really? How did you put all this together?"

"Well, to tell you the truth," Carole replies, "it wasn't all that long ago that I was sitting in an office across a desk asking questions the same way you are right now."

"So did you know from the beginning ... ?" Sue begins.

"What I wanted to do?" Carole offers. "Actually, I didn't. I just knew I liked it here and that I had more to offer than what I was doing."

"So you asked somebody for this job?" Sue inquires.

"Oh, no, this role didn't exist back then," Carole explains. "It's a long story, but I'll give you the *Cliffs Notes* version. It all changed for me when I was 38 years old. At that time, I had no idea what the future held, but I had this gnawing feeling that there had to be more for me out there—that I could be more."

Sue interrupts in an excited tone, "I know exactly what you are talking about, Carole! I feel that way, too—all the time."

"Well, then, let me pass on the best advice I ever received," says Carole. "I heard a speaker at a conference in Dallas 20 years ago, and I've never forgotten what he said. He told us it all came down to one question: Did we view our positions as a series of tasks or a series of learnings? The answer, he said, held our future.

"He went on to describe exactly what was going on inside my head," Carole continues. "I couldn't believe it. It was like he knew me. He said the reason each of us was in our particular job was not about what we could do right then, but rather it was about what we could do over time. His words rang so true for me that I resolved to look at my situation and my life at that point not as an end, but as a means to an end. I decided then and there that my real calling—here at work, at home and in life—was to keep improving, to keep growing."

"But how?" Sue asks, fascinated.

"Sue, look around," Carole explains with a sweep of her arms. "How many people do you see doing just enough to get by? They get their job description and their benefits. After that they figure out how to go through the motions on cruise control. Sue, how many people do you see making a real difference?"

"So that's what he meant?" asks Sue. "Make a difference?"

"Yes, basically, but he also told the audience how to do it," says Carole. "I don't know how many times I had heard all of this before, but on that day, in that auditorium, it was like my eyes were opened. I not only heard the words, I felt their power take a hold of my life."

Again, Sue simply asks, "How?"

Carole points to a small frame hanging on the wall. "Look over there. Read those words I have framed: 'Find a mentor, listen to your heart and take action.' Even though it's been 20 years since I first heard those words, they continue to inspire me.

"Listen to your heart," Carole repeats slowly. "No one has had your exact life experiences, so no one sees things exactly the way you do. When you experience something that generates an idea, your uniqueness powers that idea—gives it energy. If you believe in an idea, its power moves to your gut. The heart is where the ideas of your mind and the feelings in your gut come together. There, Sue, is where you should be listening for guidance. How many times has an idea about how to do something differently popped into your head?" asks Carole.

"All the time!" Sue replies.

"And how many times have you acted on those ideas? Be honest!" Carole urges.

"Well … ," Sue hesitates.

"See! That's why taking action is so important," Carole continues. "Any living thing will die if it isn't fed. For your ideas to survive, you have to feed them. Acting upon them feeds them. It breaks my heart every time I see a person of promise fail to act upon his or her ideas. You have to promise me, Sue, that the next time you have one of those moments, you'll write it down and follow up on it."

"How do I follow up? Who will listen?" Sue wonders out loud.

"For starters, I will," Carole promises.

"Ah ha!" exclaims Sue. "That's the 'find a mentor' part, right?"

"Right. And I am happy to act as your mentor—on one condition," says Carole. "That you learn to become a mentor to someone else: Pass it on. And remember, Sue, your ideas are your future. There isn't anything that can't be done better. All those ideas are out there waiting for you to discover and act upon."

~~~~~

We all have ideas—ideas about the future and ideas for our lives—but very few of us get beyond the first thought to action. We lock ourselves into where we are because of all the reasons "it won't work." Fear of failure, pride, lack of approval, insufficient funds or criticism from others—they all serve as roadblocks along our journey to keep us from moving forward.

But the fact is that despite the roadblocks, life is constantly in motion. So why not follow your instincts, trust yourself and try out some new ideas? *The question we too often find ourselves asking is, "What if it doesn't work?" The right question, however, is, "What if it does work?"*

Change begins with the simple decision to move into the driver's seat. Belief in your ideas and in your dreams must begin with a belief in yourself. Take every successful person back to his or her start and you will discover the moment when something wonderful happened. They found the courage to act. They made the decision to stop doubting and start believing. There was a moment when they combined their history, education, talents and gifts as the foundation for personal action. It was a "pivotal moment," a moment when they made a decision to act for themselves.

TRAVEL LOG TIP:
When Ellyn and I started this book, we surveyed several hundred friends and colleagues and discovered that each of them had a particular moment that affected their life tremendously. Some called it an "Ah ha!" or an "Oh wow!" Some even said they saw the light bulb pop on over their head. Someone said something to them; they noticed something; they read something—and the experience caused them to reconsider a decision and make a different choice. That choice led to a decision, which led to an action that compounded over time to produce what they now have. It can work the same way for you.   *Ken*

NOTES:

Turn Here?

Have you ever had a moment when your life changed? Maybe you were sitting in a lecture, reading a book, driving a car or listening to a conversation when suddenly, your mind started exploding with ideas and you knew life would never be the same. Each of us faces pivotal moments; they're happening all the time. And each time, we are called to action. Remember the moment when you discovered you were in love, realized your life's calling or recognized your special talents? Our decisions based on these moments define our lives. Think about driving in your car and coming to a fork in the road. Each path holds new opportunities and a different perspective. The fork provides enticing options, beckoning you to make a choice that holds the promise for great change. But the fork in the road cannot make that decision for you.

If we allow our fears to control our actions, we may find ourselves parked at that proverbial fork forever. Taking risks based on your inspirations and possibilities is what life is all about. And that action almost always involves the support of another person. Most successful people got where they are because someone helped them, believed in them and inspired them along the way. The buddy you take with you on life's road trip is the one who leans over and says, "Get behind the wheel." *When you are driving, it's your choice to turn left or right, even when the road ahead looks, as the poet Robert Frost said, "less traveled."*

TRAVEL LOG TIP:
My late husband had a tremendous influence on all the lives he touched. He taught us timeless lessons. He encouraged people to be the best they could be—never to settle. He believed in doing things right the first time. He believed in paying attention to the little things because the big stuff is so big, you'll always take care of it. He believed the only opinion that should matter to you is the opinion of the person you see every day in the mirror. If you aren't honest with that person, you won't be honest with others.   *Ellyn*

NOTES:

Everybody Starts Somewhere

We always remember the people who opened our eyes and believed in us. Often they had a contagious spirit that we couldn't help but catch. These people were genuinely passionate about seeing us succeed even when we believed we would fail. Combine that enthusiasm with their willingness to make an emotional investment in us, and it's no wonder we hold them in high regard. They gave of themselves. It doesn't matter if they were getting paid to do what they did—for example, as a teacher or a coach. What does matter is that they connected with us on a personal level. They provided "driver's ed" and rode with us for a while. And we didn't even notice the moment when they disappeared, leaving us with the strength to proceed alone.

There's really no secret to driving that route toward success. There's no magic formula that some people know, but you never will. Everyone who has achieved anything in life had to do it the same way. Their on-ramps might differ from yours, but they still had to begin by making the decision to follow their dreams and then work on those dreams every day until they came true—just like you do. *That means you have the exact same chance of success as everyone else. And it all begins with an idea.*

Most great ideas come from trying to solve a problem or trying

> **TRAVEL LOG TIP:**
> My first job out of college was with a company that promised me a career in hospital management. What I got was a chance to learn the business from what they called "the inside." I covered for whoever didn't show up that day—not in places like accounting and administration, but rather in maintenance, yard work, laundry and dishwashing. I did the job and complained about it—a lot. One day, another employee brought me a needlepoint wall hanging she had made that said, "For this I spent all those years in college?" I realized I was saying those words a lot, complaining rather than grabbing hold of the situation and doing something about it. I decided to change my attitude.   *Ken*
>
> **NOTES:**

to discover an easier or better way to do something. You start with a single thought that lays the foundation for where you want to go. The excitement you generate from allowing your dreams to multiply and grow provides the magnetism needed to pull you toward success and success toward you. Success comes from *making* something happen, from taking an idea and injecting it with action.

An ongoing process of trial and error allows you to build on your idea and work out the kinks. Walt Disney once said, "I only hope that we never lose sight of one thing —that it was all started by a mouse."[3] Walt understood the power of imagination, the power of one idea and how that one idea could lead to countless others.

> TRAVEL LOG TIP:
> The lure of the past is a product of our selective "memory." We remember what we want to and the more time passes, the better that memory looks. I have to tell you that when I was 20 I was "hot!" At least that's how I remember it. A lot of times I couldn't get a date—but I remember I was hot!   *Ken*
>
> NOTES:

Decisions, Decisions

What separates those who will succeed from those who won't—the drivers from the riders—is their willingness to draw a line in the sand that separates their life into "before" and "after." What is common to these two phases of life is the moment of separation—the moment of decision. If you have an idea or a dream, why not decide to act on it right now? Making this choice allows you to move forward and engage in future-oriented activities. *It's up to you to release the brake that holds you in place.* This new-found freedom gives you purpose and can be life changing.

Step on the gas, and the car moves. Turn the steering wheel and the car responds. In other words, action produces reaction. It's a basic scientific principle, and it's a law of human nature, too. When we act—when we *do* something—that action is based on a decision. Whether done consciously or unconsciously, deciding is easy. We make thousands of decisions about what we do every day—like when to get up, what to wear and when to speak.

The act of deciding is in perpetual motion, and many decisions compound upon one another. For example, when you decide to take a job, and that job requires a certain wardrobe, you might have to buy new clothes. From there, you have to decide how to get to and from work as well as what time to go to bed and what time to get up. All of these decisions involve making a choice. *And even when you let others make your decisions, you are still making a choice.*

> TRAVEL LOG TIP:
> In college, my roommate nicknamed me "Slick." Even at age 20, I had a vision for my life and a plan on how to achieve it. I told my dates in college, "Make no plans to get serious with me. I won't be around here long. I have places to go and things to do." We all have the inner strength to do what it takes to get to the destination we want to reach. We just need to maintain a positive can-do attitude. Don't let anybody or anything keep you out of the driver's seat.   *Ellyn*
>
> NOTES:

Choices affect outcomes. Many people don't think about this until after the fact—after time and consequences clear up any mysteries about "what happened?" Given the benefit of time, it's easy to place *other* people's decisions into categories like "good" and "bad," according to our standards. It's a very different story when it comes to judging our own decisions. *While we all have made some choices that did not move us forward, and may have caused us to move backward, we have the ability to learn from the past and change directions.*

REST STOP

Green Light!

What has happened up until now has brought you here. Honor the past and accept it with no regrets. The past need not deny you possibilities now, nor hold you down. Often the moments that bring us to our knees "jump start" us into action, motivating us to pick up the pieces and begin again. There is no such thing as failure in life; there is only learning.

Think of the past as your foundation. Now use what you are today to become what you want to be tomorrow. What you do with what *is*—that's what really matters now. Become future focused. Every moment has the potential to be pivotal and to set you on a new course destined for a new result. Making the choice to change is how we grow.

To be a person of purpose is an ambition worth striving for.

> *TRAVEL LOG TIP:*
> *I can trace each success I have experienced in my life to a specific pivotal moment. Many of these achievements are very private, and they only matter to me. The point is, however, that I can take them back to the moment they started. I can remember the first thought and how I let my mind carry it until I had a clear picture of what I wanted to do and how I would do it. The exhilaration I felt back then when I "got it" sustains me some 20 or 30 years later. I treasure those moments. They have been the steppingstones in my path through life.*   *Ellyn*

It's what we refer to as becoming passionate, on fire and filled with the drive to achieve a specific purpose that is beyond where you are today. *Discovering and accepting your purpose propels you forward.*

People with true passion are remembered for what they stood for, what they accomplished and how their lives touched others. Life passes by far too quickly for any of us to delay pursuing our passion.

Resist the often overwhelming temptation to look backwards. Okay, so you'll never be 30, or 40 or 50 again—so what? With age comes experience that inevitably broadens your perspective, if you let it. Success is blind to age. Grandma Moses was 75 when she started painting. Colonel Sanders was 65 when he started Kentucky Fried Chicken. Clara Barton founded the American Red Cross at age 60. When you open your mind to imagination and possibility, you will see that the best may, indeed, be yet to come.

Henry Ford said it well 100 years ago: "Whether you think you can or you can't, you're right!"[4] From this moment on, don't settle for less. Stretch yourself to accomplish what your head, heart and gut are telling you. If you reach for more, you will be more, do more and enrich your life.

TRAVEL PLANNING

Who are your travel partners?

When you think of your youth, what stands out in your mind as events that changed you, caused you to make an important decision or get involved with something that allowed your abilities to blossom? _____

_____

Who was the special person involved in this insight or change? _____

_____

Do you see this as your own "pivotal moment?" _____

_____

Fast forward to today: Who influences your life now? _____

_____

Whose life do you influence today? _____

_____

Do you have the "fuel" to make your journey?

What have you started but not completed to the level you had first hoped?

____ Relationships   ____ Jobs

____ Projects   ____ Other things

What stopped you from proceeding? What ideas have you put aside because it wasn't the right time in your life to follow them or develop them further? ____

_____

_____

_____

_____

_____

Is it time to act on these now? _____

_____

_____

List some other ideas that really excite you and decide if they are (1) important or not important and (2) easy to do or hard to do. For example:

	Important	Not important	Easy to do	Hard to do
Hobby				
Home improvement				
Travel				
Job				
School				
Relationships				
Community work/volunteering				
Faith community work/volunteering				
Other				

Which ideas on your list are both important and easy to do? _____

_____

_____

Look back to the Travel Planning in Chapter 1. Is there something you really wanted to do that you haven't accomplished? _____

_____

_____

_____

_____

R = RECOGNIZE
O
A
D

3

Start Your Engine!
Go Your Own Way

Mike, assistant foodservice director at a community hospital, is often asked to participate in brainstorming meetings. Despite the "rules of brainstorming," however, he's been conditioned to remain silent in these sessions because he's learned what the rules really mean:

- Speak in turns ... but let the most senior person speak first.
- Use the "parking lot" for new ideas ... but only if they support the popular idea.
- Elaborate on the ideas of others ... but make sure comments are given in descending order according to the organizational chart.
- Never say anything negative about another person's idea ... but use a lot of intimidating rhetoric to keep others' opinions in line.

This month's meeting of the hospital's morale team promises to be especially tedious for Mike because it will affect his area. The team has been charged with helping Mike come up with ideas for Halloween decorations. The human resources director, the medical records manager, the vice president of nursing, the head of hospital security, a couple of medical interns and, of course, Mike are on the team. Mike knows that in this group, he'll be low man on the totem pole.

As the meeting is called to order, neither of the two interns is present. Elizabeth Green, the vice president of nursing, immediately asserts herself, saying, "Look, we all have busy schedules and far more pressing issues than this, so let's set ourselves a maximum of 15 minutes to get something in place. Here's what I think," she fires up to steamroll. "There will be a lot of school kids visiting, so we'll have enough costumes around the place. I think that having the staff dress up is unprofessional, so let's nix that. Now, does anyone like the idea of having cake and cider for visitors at every nursing station?"

"Great idea—for nursing—but what about other departments that don't get so much visibility?" wonders the medical records person. "Besides, I've heard there's a lot of interest in the costume thing."

"I haven't heard that," the vice president replies. "Do we really want sick people seeing the hospital staff in costumes?"

Everyone is silent until the security head chimes in about the liability issues surrounding costumes. The human resources person nods her head in agreement.

"So any other comments, suggestions, ideas?" inquires the vice president. Mike is thinking about an idea and mustering the courage to offer something when the vice president says, "Three, two, one—okay, then, it's settled. We'll have cake and cider at every nursing station. It will be expensed to hospital administration. Other departments can see if they have room in their own budgets for similar activities. Mike can do the food, and you guys can contact him yourselves. Sound good? Great. Well, that was only 8 minutes, everybody. Good meeting. Thanks."

As the participants leave the table, Mike grabs his empty legal pad and heads to the door. He is frustrated because he hasn't said what he feels.

"Oh, Mike, can you stay a few minutes?" the vice president asks. He turns to her and smiles. "Perhaps she is going to ask my opinion," he thinks.

"Mike," she says, "there are a couple of things I wanted to let you know. We've all noticed that you don't take these meetings off on tangents like you've done in the past. You're developing into a nice manager."

Mike feels his stomach sink but manages a weak smile. "And by the way," she continues, "remember that we have 22 nursing units on three shifts. So be sure you make enough food so no one runs out. Okay?"

Sixty-six cakes means a lot of last-minute work, but Mike knows his team can handle it; they're up to last-minute demands. Mike nods and leaves the room with some familiar thoughts and feelings knocking around in his head: "Why am I working here? What is the point of being considered a manager when I don't feel like one? It's silly to think anyone will notice a person like me who doesn't have alphabet soup behind his name in this place where it's all about medicine and medical degrees."

Mike thinks about quitting. He's thought about it before but knows he probably never will. Benefits at the hospital are simply too good. Tonight, he'll have plenty of time to think about what he should do; he has swapped hours with the evening manager and will be working late.

Later that evening, Mike gives the cashier a break and covers her station. Business is slow and the place is clean.

"Hey, Mike, how are you doing?" asks Dr. Kelly Larsen, who is standing at the cash register with her evening meal. Dr. Larsen is an intern working the intensive care rotation and pulling late hours. She's been at the hospital about a year. She always engages Mike in conversation and he likes how she treats him—more like a friend than a "servant," which is how he often feels as a foodservice employee.

"Hi, Dr. Kelly, I'm good. You?" Mike replies.

"Well, it looks like I am probably doing somewhat better than you," observes Dr. Larsen. "Why the long face tonight? You look like you are a million miles away. Sorry Dr. Bishop and I missed the team meeting today. I slept through it and Joe was in surgery."

"Oh no, I know your schedules are crazy," Mike assures her.

"So what happened?" Dr. Larsen asks. "Any new, exciting ideas or did Liz Green from nursing control the whole thing like she usually does?"

"Yeah, you pretty much nailed it," says Mike.

"So, Mike, what's the plan?" Dr. Larsen asks.

"There isn't one. Just cider and cake at the nursing stations—same thing we've been doing every year since I got here," Mike laments.

"Oh, gosh, we play that same tape every holiday," Dr. Larsen observes. "I thought you were going to share some of those big ideas of yours?"

"I was about to when Liz complimented me for keeping quiet. After that, I chickened out," Mike admits.

"Mike, you know as well as I do that the only people who will see that cake and cider thing are Liz Green's employees," Dr. Larsen says. "That's 20 people per station. And how many thousands of employees work in this hospital? The cafeteria is the place where people come for a break. We need to have some fun right here."

"I was going to say something," Mike assures her, "but all the department heads had pretty much decided what they were going to do. So I thought, 'Who's going to listen to me?' I just work in the kitchen."

Dr. Larsen looks Mike in the eye and slowly repeats his words: "Is that right? You just work in the kitchen? Is that how you really feel, or are you just a little hesitant about spreading your wings in that group? Let me ask you a question someone asked me when I first started medical school: What is the most important organ in the body?"

"Well," Mike thinks a minute, "I guess I would have to say the brain—or maybe the heart."

"Those organs are certainly important," concedes Dr. Larsen, "but how long do you think a body would survive if it didn't have a liver to filter the blood or if both lungs shut down? Or if you could no longer eat?"

"Well, then, I guess the answer is that every organ is important," Mike concludes, "each for different reasons."

"Exactly," Dr. Larsen confirms. "Do you see what I am getting at? Every organization is like the human body; no one is more important than anyone else. So letting a bunch of people tell you what your department needs to do is like the feet telling the hands how to work.

"So, let's replay that meeting," she says. "I know those people and I know they have important jobs—but so do you. And I'll tell you something—of all of them, you are the one who sees every employee every day. When it comes to morale issues, that group should listen to you. So if it were your call, what would you do with this cafeteria for Halloween?"

"Oh, that's easy," Mike replies eagerly. "First, I would change the menu—not adding new food items, just changing the names of things so they sounded scary. I'd dial the lights down and play some Halloween music through the paging system. I'd decorate with a lot of orange and black and give every customer a homemade treat."

"Good!" exclaims Dr. Larsen. "Then that's exactly what you should do. Who's stopping you? Here's another idea: When I was in med school, the cafeteria had a pumpkin-carving contest. It was a hoot."

"That would be cool," Mike says.

"You can still do it," Dr. Larsen asserts. "Get some pumpkins right now and take them around to the units. Night shift people can work on them."

"I'll call the early crew," Mike says, "and ask them to start planning their costumes, and I'll have one of them stop on the way to work to pick up a bunch of candy."

"Now you're talking, Mike," says Dr. Larsen, "I can't wait to see how it all turns out!"

"Thanks for the ideas, Dr. Kelly," Mike replies.

"What are you thanking me for?" Dr. Larsen asks. "Give yourself some credit. Those good ideas were percolating inside you all along! Remember if you don't stand for something, you'll fall for anything!"

~~~~~

Consider that your fingerprints, your voiceprint and your DNA are all traceable to you alone. No one else is or ever will be exactly like you. And because of your unique experiences, no one will ever have your life perspective or your exact dreams.

Motivational author Stephen Covey is known for many clever observations, and one in particular is, "Everything in life is created twice."[5] In other words, physical creation always follows mental creation—the idea. Walt Disney believed, "If you can dream it, you can do it," and so should we.[6]

The most important ingredient in the creative process is imagination. *The best way to do just about everything hasn't been thought of yet.* Taking time each day to work through your ideas is an essential step on the road to success. You've probably heard people say they get their best ideas in the shower—maybe that's true for you. Unfortunately, most of us don't have the luxury of taking long idea-infused showers. There's just not enough time in the day. But can you imagine how many good ideas you'd have if you let your mind wander 30, 40 or even just 10 minutes more a day? Successful people aren't always the smartest folks in the crowd, but you can bet they are the ones who allow themselves the time and space to think.

TRAVEL LOG TIP:
In the late 1970s, when I decided I wanted to start a foodservice software company, my brother told me I was crazy—that I didn't know the difference between hardware and software. My reply to him was, "Neither does anyone I will be selling to."   *Ellyn*

NOTES:

TRAVEL LOG TIP:
We come face to face with opportunities every day but don't act on them until we are ready. I never look at the possibility of failure. I only look at the possibility of learning something new. In reality, we never fail, we are just experiencing life!   *Ellyn*

NOTES:

And when they have an idea, they focus on it and act.

Every day we make choices, and those choices affect our lives both personally and professionally. It doesn't matter if your choices concern a life decision such as getting married or a business decision. Where you go and what you do are *your* choices. In the end, you have to take control of your life and make sure you are going in a direction that leads to your goal. Consider all the facts in the decision-making process, but more importantly, listen to your heart and let your conscience be your guide.

TRAVEL LOG TIP:
We must strive to be better, work smarter and be more politically savvy. Winners are not necessarily smarter or stronger, but they are willing to go the extra mile. Winners know how to read a situation and get through it.
Ellyn

NOTES:

Step on the Gas!

Forward momentum is fueled by a positive attitude, belief in yourself and a passion to succeed. Excuses and rationalization bring forward momentum to a screeching halt. So why do we allow anything to get in the way and block our progress? If you truly are in control of your own destiny—and we believe that you are—you have the power to accomplish what is important to you. You have the power to live your *own* dream. Not someone else's. Your own. This is the difference between driving versus just riding along.

TRAVEL LOG TIP:
I was raised in a modest, hard-working family in the Deep South. I began working at a very young age—babysitting, picking and selling pecans, and working weekends in a department store. I made my own clothes and the only time I can recall going out to dinner at a restaurant was once a year on my birthday. But I knew that was not going to be my life forever.
Ellyn

NOTES:

Resolve to set your alarm clock to go off 30 to 60 minutes before you really need to get up. Use that time to think, plan and mull over the day ahead, or just let your mind wander, exploring new ideas and possibilities. If you are like most people, you aren't scheduling any private time like this. You'll be surprised how productive an early morning "think session" can be. It's not like yoga or meditation, during which you are trying to be devoid of thought. On the contrary, a think session is time for you to embark on a personal journey. If you like a scenario that passes through your mind, grab it and start developing a plan.

TRAVEL LOG TIP:
I worked hard in school, became involved in community organizations and developed friendships with accomplished women I looked up to. I looked beyond. I knew one day I would be able to turn opportunities into success. To this day, I try to place in my mind a picture of who I want to be and how I am going to get there. I never stop thinking, dreaming, planning. *Ellyn*

NOTES:

And the bigger the dream, the better, right? The more you allow your dreams to unfold, the more possibilities emerge. By giving your imagination free rein, you can "try on" different scenarios without making a commitment. Sounds like a great deal—maximum possibility from minimal investment, just a commitment to the fantasy and trust in yourself.

By thinking and talking about our dreams, they take on a life of their own. Have you ever heard someone say they wanted something so bad they could almost "taste it?" That kind of passion is what we are talking about here. When you live and breathe your dreams, it really doesn't matter what anyone else thinks. In fact, most people spend entirely too much time trying to please others. When you accept that your life is about you—when you allow yourself to be happy and fulfilled—things take a powerful turn. Your confidence and self-esteem will increase as you become more centered and grounded. While this new mindset may seem self-centered, the end result is quite the opposite. In fact, you will become a better spouse, partner, parent, friend, boss and/or employee.

Be Your Own Best Friend

Self-esteem comes from the continuous affirmation that you are "okay." When you are young, your parents provide this validation. As you grow older, you rely on friends, teachers, colleagues and bosses. When you don't receive validation from someone else, you must rely on yourself. Just because someone else doesn't buy into your dreams doesn't mean you should not move forward. In fact, the sooner you let go of expectations that others will or should buy into your dreams, the better! After all, no one else can make your dreams a reality; only you can. It's your road trip.

Greatness comes to the risk takers, to those who believe in themselves, and believe that what they want to accomplish is both important and possible. Are you ready to make a decision and take a stand—one that has at its core a fundamental belief in yourself? Naturally, there will be roadblocks along the way; be ready to go around, over or even through them. Many of the roadblocks you will face, however, you yourself will create by making excuses, procrastinating and simply wasting time.

Don't cheat yourself. Cut out the things in your life that drain your energy and your time and keep you from growing. If you want

TRAVEL LOG TIP:
Over the years, I have found that when I share my ideas with others, everybody has an opinion about what I should do. For me, what's important is that I listen to my heart and my gut and that ultimately I believe in myself and what I am trying to accomplish. I listen to the advice of others, but I keep it in context—it's their opinion. My passion was for business and management and working with people. To do that, I had to listen to myself first. I had a lot of critics in the early years, but my "I'll show them" attitude has paid off with big dividends. It is much easier to give up than to go for the big win. Have the courage to take the ride.　　*Ellyn*

NOTES:

to change professions, get moving. If you want to go back to school, sign up. If you want to have a loving relationship, make time for it. There is no secret formula for success, just a process people have been using for years. Watch those you admire and do what they do.

W.A.T.C.H.

Watch
Achievers
Then
Copy (their)
Habits

TRAVEL PLANNING

How far can you go?

If you knew there was no possibility of failure, how bold would you be? _____

_____

_____

_____

Where would you go? What would you do? _____

_____

_____

_____

Do you know yourself?

Everyone has characteristics that make him or her unique. What are yours?

____ Creative   ____ Good parenting skills

____ Good business sense   ____ Great friend

____ Good networking skills   ____ Can keep a secret

____ Helpful to others

____ High level of community involvement and respect

____ Communication ability – written, oral, listening

____ Others: _____

_____

Are you willing to make a personal commitment to go for a walk or sit in a park or even in your own back yard just to let your mind wander—and then write down what you want to accomplish next month, next year or whatever time-frame you chose?

If so, sign here: _____

How will you overcome the obstacles in your path?

As you anticipate taking action on your new ideas, what obstacles do you see that might prevent you from giving your idea full attention? Consider how you could overcome these obstacles when they appear.

Job _____

_____

_____

Family responsibilities _____

_____

_____

Activity commitments _____

_____

_____

Lack of sleep _____

_____

_____

Difficulty scheduling time for yourself _____

_____

_____

Others _____

_____

_____

R
A
D

O = OPTIMIZE

Section 2

"Time is the coin of your life. Be careful lest you let other people spend it for you."
—Carl Sandburg, poet

Go for It!

 There's No Turning Back.

 Be Careful!

 Bright Idea!

 Pause and Consider.

 Stop!

 Turn It Around.

4

Rules of the Road
You Can Get There from Here

Joyce is nervous. It's her turn to make a presentation to her class. She understands her subject—"Leadership: Involving Every Team Member in Determining a Successful Strategy"—but she is apprehensive about her peers. Many of them have completed their presentations, and the classroom atmosphere has changed. It is more difficult for the students to focus, and several of the student instructors have had a hard time keeping control of the class. Joyce knows that presenting before her peers and holding their attention will take all her strength and talent.

Joyce stands at the front of the room, gripping the podium as her peers brush past her to find their seats. She begins by announcing the title of the presentation. Immediately, the students break into two groups: one that supports her leadership style and one that doesn't.

Joyce asks everyone in class to gather their things, leave the room and wait in the hallway. She asks for silence out of respect for the other classes in session and tells her classmates that she will join them in the hallway in about five minutes.

When Joyce comes back to retrieve her class, she tells them in a low voice that when they go back into the classroom, they will notice that the desks have been reset in circles. Each group of circles is for a team and each team's membership is limited to the number of seats available in the circle. The name of each team is written on a sign placed on one of the desks in each circle. Joyce gives her students the next 2 minutes to choose their team and take their seats.

An excited energy takes over as the students move inside and see their team choices: budget, transportation, participants, lodging, local activities and destination. Once everyone is seated, Joyce says, "All right, teams, here is your assignment. We are going on a vacation, and certain decisions must be made. Each team has been given the data it needs to make the decision it is responsible for, and that is the only decision the team can make. You can have no influence over any other team's work. I suggest you take the next 20 minutes to review the data. Be prepared to ask any questions you need to in order to make the right call for your team. Go!"

Joyce excuses herself from the room and sits in a chair just outside the door. She hears a lively exchange going on inside—so lively, in fact, that in about 15 minutes she walks back into the classroom to check on the students' progress. "How's it going?" she asks. Her question is answered by 30 voices protesting at the same time. "Wait a minute," she exclaims. "One spokesperson for each team, please. Now ... what's the issue?"

"Joyce," one student replies, "none of us can decide anything without some information from the other teams."

"All right," Joyce says, "I am going to ask the spokesperson of each team to step out into the hallway. The rest of you keep your cool." In the hallway, Joyce instructs the team leaders that they can have one new piece of information and they must decide amongst themselves what that one piece should be. She tells them to come back in once they have determined the most important piece of information everyone needs to proceed.

Joyce then returns to the classroom and informs the students that the team leaders have agreed to seek out one new piece of information. When the team leaders return, she asks, "What is it you want to know?"

Deb speaks up first. "We need to know the destination. None of us can do any planning until we know where we are going."

"Okay, destination team," Joyce says, "I provided you with research on the most popular destinations in the country. Where are we headed?"

The destination spokesperson replies, "Well, we couldn't decide." The other students groan in unison. "Hang on. Hear me out," he continues. "Each of us is so passionate about our choice that the only fair way to decide is with a lottery. We placed our choices in this hat and I will draw one now. Okay," he says holding a piece of paper up for all to see, "it appears that we are going to Orlando, Florida."

The teams get right back to work. Joyce observes the interaction for several minutes and then asks the team leaders to meet her in the hallway again.

"Okay, everyone," she says, "I'll give you the opportunity to ask another question. Come back in when you are ready."

They return almost immediately. "We need to know how much money we will have to spend," one of the leaders says.

"Budget team, you have that data," Joyce says. "How much do we have in the pot?"

"Our data say that the average family of four in America spends about $5,000 for two weeks in Orlando," the budget spokesperson reports, "so we are going to set the total budget for this trip at $1,250 per person."

The participation spokesperson chimes in, "We decided that all 30 of us in the class will be participating. At $1,250 each, that's $47,500."

"Destination, budget and participation teams—you have done your work," Joyce affirms. "Head to the hallway. The rest of us will stay behind and make some more decisions. Let's see, all we have left are the transportation, lodging and activities. It's up to you three teams to figure the rest out."

"It says in the flight book that the average Chicago to Orlando round trip is running $440 these days," offers the budget spokesperson.

The attractions team spokesperson adds, "An average Disney World ticket is $60, but we can get a three-day hopper pass for $140."

"Let's see," recounts Joyce, "we have $47,500 to spend and with flights at $440, that means travel for 30 people is going to cost $13,200. We have $34,300 left. The three-day hopper pass for everyone will total $8,400. That leaves us $25,900 for two weeks. Accommodations team, what does an average hotel stay in Orlando cost?"

"We can stay right on a Disney property at a moderate-class resort for about $70 per night double occupancy," the accommodations spokesperson says.

Joyce tallies the tab so far: "So we have 14 nights at $70 per night, which is $980 times 15 rooms. That's $14,700. So now we have $11,200 left for meals for two weeks. That's $168 per person per week for food. That seems okay, doesn't it? It's about $9 per meal."

A lively discussion ensues among the students:

"$9 per meal is okay if all you want to do the whole time you are there is hit one park for three days. There is so much to do; it doesn't quite seem fair."

"Maybe we could cut out a meal per day?"

"No, that isn't going to work. People have to eat."

"Hey, look at this. It says here that Amtrak offers a Chicago to Orlando train that takes two days but round trip is only $205."

"Two days up and two days back would save us four hotel nights per person."

"Let's figure that out. $205 per person is $6,350 versus the $13,200 the plane was going to cost. And with four fewer nights in Orlando, our room charge would drop from $14,700 to $10,500."

"What does that leave us per person if we keep the hopper passes in?"

The budget spokesperson runs the numbers. "$47,500 minus Amtrak, rooms and park tickets leaves us with $25,350."

"If we added another tour, maybe Universal, for $200 total, we'd still have $19,350," he says. "That's $967.50 per person per week or about $109.60 for food and miscellaneous expense per day. I think we've done it."

When the class reconvenes, Joyce has the team spokespersons report the result of his or her team's work. There is some groaning over the Amtrak decision, but it is quickly drowned out as the students realize they have planned a trip to a fun town with a realistic entertainment and food budget for two weeks.

As the class wraps up, Joyce asks for feedback on the process. The students comment on how quickly things happened when they accepted their roles and got out of the way of others. They say they see that breaking into teams made sense. Lots of comments focus on feeling involved in the decision-making. When Joyce asks the class to name the single most important lesson they have learned, all agree it's that nothing can happen until you know where you are going.

~~~~~

You are the common element between where you are today and where you want to be tomorrow. So isn't it ironic that in your efforts to move ahead in life, you yourself often construct the barriers that prevent you from progressing. If you have yet to accomplish your goals, perhaps you're simply not allowing yourself the room to move toward where you want to be. A boss shows respect for and trust in an employee by being direct, making the necessary resources available and then getting out of the way. *When you respect and believe in yourself, you get out of your own way!* That's what we mean by "optimize," harnessing the best option because you can make your own choices. Clear the path to enable yourself to function at your best, be effective and *move forward toward your dream.*

Caught in a Traffic Rotary

Often the most difficult part of moving forward is getting out of the activity traps we make for ourselves. It's like being in a traffic rotary; once you're caught going round and round, it's hard to break out. That's why creating a dream or future vision is so important. It locks you into your destination. Having a strong belief and being passionate about pursuing that belief is how you pull your future toward you. Like using a GPS (global positioning satellite) system, you must first program in your destination. The system can't function if it doesn't know where you want to go.

TRAVEL LOG TIP:
Every day I sit at my desk and ask myself, "What can I do today to bring me closer to my goals?" People who really want to be successful will do whatever it takes. They can picture what they want and they make it happen. They do research and write a plan. They share the plan with friends and colleagues. If they run into an obstacle, they figure out how to get around or over it. It takes faith, courage and perseverance to make dreams a reality. Nothing happens by accident. Even winning the lottery takes buying a ticket.   *Ellyn*

NOTES:

When you take on new, future-focused activities, the here-and-now must be reevaluated. Deciding what to let go of can be tough. More than 40 years ago, President John F. Kennedy addressed the American people with these immortal words, "Change is the law of life, and those who look only to the past, or to the present, are certain to miss the future."[7]

His words still challenge us today because in clinging to the methods that created success for us in the past, we interfere with achieving our goals in the future. *The same is true for the activity traps we find ourselves in today.* In other words, the only way you can accomplish a new goal is by embracing a new way of do-ing things. In order to over-come your fear of change, you must confront that fear. That means grabbing control of your time right now. Set your priorities according to the future you envision for yourself—that's optimizing!

If you allow the activity traps of today to stop you from moving toward your goal, you will find yourself planning for tomorrow by accumulating ideas instead of results. You can smooth out the road ahead by redis-tributing or eliminating any activities that are not lead-ing you to your goals. Con-sider that GPS system gizmo again: It will never lead you off on a road that doesn't lead to your destination. Put an end to the redundancy in your life! Stop doing things just for the sake of doing

TRAVEL LOG TIP:
I can take the process of writing this book back to the instant I set myself on the path. It's been a journey of more than 12 years. What started as a dream became real as I built my skill set. I found my true inspiration in being with people, speaking to them and hear-ing their reactions to my ideas. That is what motivated me and kept me on the path. There were many times I wondered if I could do it. Each affir-mation brought me back to my initial passion. The easiest thing to do would have been to give up and, believe me, I wanted to sometimes. If you find your-self frustrated it's okay to take a break, but never stop. That's the art of pur-suit. As long as you are working toward a goal you believe in, you will have the energy to move forward. Ken

NOTES:

them. You can only go around the block so many times. Take control. Learn to say the scary word *NO!*

The 'Art of Pursuit'

Most of us let our dreams drift through our minds as if we were driving through a fog. We simply can't see where we're going. Learning the art of pursuit will help you burn off that fog of confusion. Practicing the art of pursuit helps you make your dreams your reality that much faster. First, you need to have a firm concept of where you want to be. Picture your dream. Feel it. Touch it. Visualization is a wonderful way to add life to your dreams. For example, imagine you are just finishing college; go to a graduation ceremony in your mind and picture yourself receiving that diploma. Hold on to that image, and find a way to experience it every day. If you want to travel and see the world, but your budget won't stretch to make it possible, keep travel posters and brochures on hand as a reminder to save the pennies that will add up to the dollars you need.

TRAVEL LOG TIP:
About 3 miles from where I was living, there was a huge gravel pit that had filled itself in with spring-fed water. Rumor had it that a developer would one day turn it into a bona fide lake and build luxury homes around it. For years, I used to drive out there on weekends and walk around, imagining what it would be like to live there. I didn't have two nickels to rub together, but I had imagination. My wife and I scoured magazines for ideas and eventually had an architect draw up some plans. One day, we took the plans over to the area and imagined what our home would look like—the layout, the landscaping, the lake, the beach, the kids playing. Later, before the road improvements were even in, I got into a conversation with the developer about our dream house. He called me a week later and offered us our choice of lots!   *Ken*

NOTES:

Making your dreams come true takes more than good intentions. It takes commitment. It takes setting and keeping priorities. *Deciding what is really important brings you face to face with some difficult choices.* It's always

easier to leave things as they are. But, of course, nothing will ever change if you don't change your activity. As Benjamin Franklin once said, "The definition of insanity is doing the same thing over and over and expecting different results."[8]

Once a decision is made, only action will move you toward accomplishing your goal. Commit yourself each day to working on what makes you feel whole, what makes you feel that you are living life to the fullest in pursuit of your dream. You have already taken the first step: You are reading this book. Determine to make changes. *Keep moving!*

TRAVEL PLANNING
No time to spare!

What commitments have you made in the past that you probably wouldn't make today? _____

_____

_____

_____

_____

What commitments would you like to make now? _____

_____

_____

_____

_____

Make a list of what you do every day for a week. At the end of the week, look at your list and determine what is really important. What is moving you toward your life goal? _____

_____

_____

_____

_____

What changes can you make? _____

_____

_____

_____

_____

How can you consolidate? _____

_____

_____

_____

_____

_____

_____

_____

_____

Can you give up unnecessary tasks? _____

_____

_____

_____

_____

_____

_____

_____

List three activities that you do daily or weekly that can be eliminated or given to someone else to handle. _____

_____

_____

_____

_____

_____

_____

_____

_____

5

Merging Traffic
Keep Your Eye on the Road

Franco is excited. Who wouldn't be? After 20 years in the work-a-day world, things are finally going his way. He has discovered the secret to success that has eluded him all these years. And now that he knows it, he is going to make darn sure he uses it.

He can smile about it now, but thinking back on his life, he realizes that he had become a follower—a good person who did what he was told. He followed his pack of peers when he was younger because he wanted to avoid making waves. The advice of his adult peers shaped the course of his life, a life that somehow ended up quite different from what he had once dreamed it would be.

He could recall a time when he had almost broken free. He was in junior high school when, on a cold day in November, he discovered an old saxophone in his parents' attic. He felt a strong desire to play the instrument and subsequently fell in love with music. After he pestered his parents, he was allowed to take music lessons. He studied the sax and along the way taught himself how to play guitar as well. Soon he was playing in a band, and a new side of him emerged—an artsy side.

After high school, Franco went to college, earning his way through by playing nights and weekends with his band. He had wanted to study music in college, but his parents told him there was no way he could ever make a living with music. In the end, he lost the battle, left the band, put his instruments aside and decided to study business.

His first job out of college was an "entry-level" position that threw him together with a group of gruff individuals. He hated the job, and it lasted only about two weeks. Next, an appraisal company hired him to process loans. Franco sat in a cubicle all day and did tedious work.

About a year later, Franco found a job with an expediting company that distributed widgets all over the country. He started in the warehouse, was promoted into trucking and then moved into the office to manage a bunch of file folders. When he was hired, he was told to "trust the company to do what was best for him"—so he did. Unfortunately, for six years, the company thought that the best thing for Franco was to change his title and location every six months. He moved himself and his family nine times because someone in the company thought it was necessary for Franco's professional development.

Franco found himself working a job that was quickly chopping years off his life, a job for which he felt no passion. In his daydreams, Franco would consider other options, but these dreams were always tempered by the well-intentioned warnings of others: Do this. Don't do that. Take this job. Attend this function. Stay low on the radar. Become more visible, etc.

Maria, Franco's wife, who had fallen in love with the idealistic dreamer she had met in college, saw her husband's spirit slowly dying. As she supported him from one change to the next, she watched her "Frankie" become more and more a follower. And to make matters worse, somewhere along the line, Franco lost touch with the music that had once inspired him.

One day, well into his 40s, Franco had a life-changing experience. A person whose advice he had followed for 10 years confided something to him. Early in her career, she confessed, she had made some bad choices. She had disliked her job and had become as frustrated as he was with where things were headed in her life. She vented to Franco that she hated where she was, and as far as being a leader was concerned, she never spent any time worrying about her employees' futures. She was too caught up worrying about her own.

Franco was speechless. This was an epiphany. He had spent all those years being a good soldier, following orders and directions. He had given more credence to the thoughts of others than he did to his own inclinations and feelings. Why had he done that? Why hadn't he just believed in himself?

It was hard not to be depressed by these realizations. Franco had spent years listening to everyone else—coaches, teachers, family members and bosses—when they probably were as confused as he was. He made a decision then and there to silence the "voices." And in the midst of this moment of clarity, he remembered a life lesson he had learned years before from his youngest daughter, now a grown woman in college.

She had taken his hand in hers and said, "Dad, haven't you always told us to follow our hearts? It's time for you to practice what you preach. We want you to be happy doing what you love to do. The rest will take care of itself."

It took Franco a while to rekindle his passion for music. He still went into work everyday, but each day found him with more pep in his step. He found a quote he liked and placed a framed copy on his desk: "If it's going to be, it's up to me."

He woke up a little earlier every day, excited to use that time to record his thoughts like he used to. In the evenings, he took out his old guitar and found that he hadn't lost all of his skills. He listened to more music, attended concerts and even tried his hand at writing some songs. Franco began enjoying himself, living a life in which he took a little more control of the clock every day. As he did, he grew back into a man of which he was proud.

Now Franco is starting to set things right, to break away from the pack and seek out adventure on his own. Now every day is his independence day. He is ready. His thoughts, ideas and dreams will no longer remain tucked away. For the first time in a long time, Franco feels inspired.

~~~~~

When you start believing that what *is* happening is all that *can* happen, it's time for a change! It wasn't all that long ago that the possibilities in your life seemed endless, right? Then reality set in and with it came a long list of expectations (yours and "theirs"). The debt, job, family, house and car, became two cars, a bigger house, more debt, and more work. The cycle never dies. What started out as a promise for a better life soon turned into a lot of empty promises—in large part made to yourself. Along that road, "work to live" became "live to work"—harder, faster and longer than everybody else.

When we live just to keep up, we borrow from the future by paying for the past with the work of the present.

Each new responsibility we add to our life brings its own agenda along for the ride—the things we have to have, places we have to be, people we have to be there for, and work we have to do to pay for it all. Every change in one dimension of life creates the need for adjustments in other dimensions. And these changes never happen one at a time, do they? Life comes at you from all sides. And before you know it, you're creeping along in low gear with your hand on the emergency brake, ready to pull at any time.

For some of us, it is difficult to break free—to break away from the tape that keeps repeating in our mind. But the fact remains that you have the ultimate choice. Grab the wheel. You have control over what you do,

TRAVEL LOG TIP:
When my children were younger, even 5 or 6 years old, I shared dreams with them and what I was doing to accomplish my goals. As they got older, I took them on business trips with me, and I invited them to my presentations. Today, my children are adults. They are still involved in sharing my dreams, and now they are helping to make them happen. In addition, I think I have influenced them to be successful in their own lives. As parents, teachers, coaches, clergy, etc., we need to remember the impact our example can have. *Ellyn*

NOTES:

what you say, and how you act and interact. Be careful not to box yourself into a routine. *If you lock yourself in the slow lane, all you can do is watch people in the fast lane get there quicker.*

Who's Coming Along for the Ride?

Take a look at the people around you. It should be clear that some of them are keeping you right where you are, while others are working to inspire you and move you ahead. People react predictably to new ideas. Some get it and are willing to jump on board; some say they get it but are reluctant to change; and some just never get it—ever.

We've all had the experience of presenting an idea to someone and having that person throw cold water on it. We can be discouraged and give up, or find someone else who thinks the idea is the greatest thing they've ever heard. Those naysayers are sometimes people who are closest to us—like family members, friends and coworkers. You have to ask yourself: Do they really know what's best for me? Do they just not want to see me get hurt? Or do they simply want to hold me in place?

TRAVEL LOG TIP:
I marvel at my young nephew who dropped out of engineering school to pursue his dream of becoming a chef. He wanted to attend culinary school but decided to work for a year in the kitchens of different restaurants to get a better understanding of operations, techniques and preparation styles. He realized that becoming a chef doesn't happen over night. None of us can put ourselves in the middle of a new project and immediately know what to do. Our ability to learn is based on doing, seeing, reading, and experiencing. Going through the process serves a purpose.   *Ellyn*

NOTES:

Now think about the people who always encouraged you. We often remember a favorite teacher or boss or a special friend. Instead of offering a pail of water to douse our ideas, they gave us a can of gas to fuel our dreams. If you are going to seek input, make sure it's from a variety of sources. Then surround yourself with the people who inspire you to keep going. They are the ones who are so empowering that we are drawn to them repeatedly. Invite them along for the ride.

Although bookstores are full of inspirational stories about so called self-made men and women, there is a common thread to all of their success. These people have achieved by learning how to involve others in their dreams. And as their dreams took shape, they knew to add people with different skills and perspectives as needed.

TRAVEL LOG TIP:
In my company, we pride ourselves on promoting from within the organization. One of our success stories is about a married mother of three young sons who is our controller. She began working for us more than 7 years ago as an accounting clerk. She wanted more out of her job and kept asking for additional responsibilities. A few years back, she shared with me that she dreamed about going back to school, but since she married young and had three children, her dream had been on hold. "Why don't you go to school?" I suggested. "Let's change your schedule so you can tackle at least one class a semester." And that is exactly what she is doing. *Ellyn*

NOTES:

Driving solo can make for a long trip, but having a trusted friend beside you can make the journey a lot more pleasant. Start with the people around you now. Share your aspirations and your dreams and listen to theirs. Create the opportunity for them to see your light at the end of the tunnel—and for you to see theirs as well. Everyone will benefit, but someone has to turn the key to ignite the process. Getting started is the hardest part for most people. We can talk ourselves out of taking that next step, but if we share our idea with someone who encourages us, getting started isn't nearly as scary. *So get out there now and find someone with that "can-of-gas" enthusiasm that's going to drive you to move forward.*

Who's Got the Best Directions?

As for those who are holding you back or in place, put their negative energy into perspective. In every circle of family, friends, acquaintances and co-workers, there are the naysayers and the people who are afraid to take risks. Although they don't share your vision, remember that their opinions come from their own life experiences, which, of course, are different from yours. In addition, not everyone who expresses his or her opinion has your best interest in mind. In fact, most people will act in their own self-interest. Negative behavior from others, such as displaying a cynical attitude or hurling insults and put-downs, is meant to keep you moving at their speed.

Imagine a continuum with you in the middle and the other people in your life falling on either side of you. You'll know where they belong by how they react to you. The avoiders are at one end of the continuum. They will look past who you are and what's going on with you. Avoiders who are closer to you may be more vocal in their attempts to hold you back. At the other end of the continuum are the acceptors. These people accept your reality. The more vocal people among the acceptors will work with you to pull you forward. Can you place the people you interact with regularly on this continuum?

Avoiders ◄——————— YOU ———————► Acceptors
(Hold you back)   (Push you forward)

Not everyone in your life is going to join your team, but don't let that stop you. *Be on the lookout for moments when others are trying to hold you back because of their own insecurities.* Steer clear of them and stay tuned to the calm rational voice that encourages you to follow your path and your conscience. If you have a gut feeling that something's not right, listen to it! In time, even the naysayers will get out of the way because of how strong you've become in trusting yourself.

When you seek out someone else's opinion, look for an expert—someone knowledgeable about the pros and cons of what you want to do. Consider what the experts have to say but take personal responsibility for the final decision. It takes a lot of inner strength and self-confidence to give yourself permission to do what is important to you.

TRAVEL PLANNING
Get around those roadblocks!

What obstacles have you faced in life that you have been able to overcome?

Job _____

_____

School _____

_____

Relationships _____

_____

Community _____

_____

Are there people or circumstances that are holding you back from what you would like to accomplish? _____

_____

Has anyone ever told you that you could not do something? Do you remember how you felt? _____

_____

Were you able to prove them wrong? If so, how did that feel? _____

_____

Who is in your "you can do it" club? Make a list. _____

_____

_____

_____

_____

_____

_____

6

Draw Yourself a New Map

No Shortcuts Allowed!

The man entering the auditorium is a success. With each step he takes toward the podium, he exudes grace and confidence.

As he moves along, he seems to assess the audience, smiling at those to his left and right, then turning to greet those seated in the balcony. The cheers and applause die down as he raises a hand to silence the crowd. He sweeps his gaze across his audience and seems to meet the eyes of every person seated before him.

"I wonder," he begins, "which one of you is the person I came here to speak with tonight?" In the audience, Yvonne reaches over, rests her hand upon her husband's arm and gives it a gentle squeeze. Louis knows what it means. He knows why he is here. He knows Yvonne wants him to be the one, yet he has his doubts.

"Let me ask you a question," the speaker says, "with a show of hands, how many of you have come here seeking a different path for your life than the one you are on?" Everyone in the audience raises his or her hand high.

"Excellent!" he exclaims. "Now, how many of you can tell me that you have a burning desire in your heart to do something more meaningful with your life?" Again, virtually everyone in the audience raises his or her hand. "Good," the speaker says. "Please keep your hands up only if you promise to answer my next question truthfully." While many audience members snicker, only a few actually put their arms down.

"Here it comes," the speaker warns, "and consider well what I am asking. Who among you has developed and is acting upon a written plan for the next five years of your life—a plan that you would be willing to share with the rest of the audience if I called upon you to come up on this stage?"

As he walks off the stage into the audience, hands quickly fall. People squirm in their seats and many lower their eyes to avoid meeting his.

"Where has all your enthusiasm gone?" he wonders aloud. "Where are the hands now? In this whole auditorium, I can only see about 20 people trying to get my attention. Ladies and gentlemen, please look at those who have their hands held high. Memorize their faces. You will see each of these people again. I can assure you that these are the people who are well on their way to success. In fact, I can guarantee they will not only achieve their desires but exceed them."

Yvonne and Louis are not among that group.

As the speaker returns to the stage, he continues, "Let me tell you who specifically I came here for tonight. It's not those few of you who volunteered a minute ago. You're just here for a little validation. I came for one of you who didn't raise his or her hand.

"You know who you are," he continues. "You're the one who really doesn't know what's going to happen next, and you're just praying for some answers. You're the one who feels close to your wits end. Is that you? You have worked hard in life, yet feel you're missing out on so much more —not just material possessions—but that sense of calm that emanates from those who have discovered how to live a confident life. Is this you? If it is, here's some good news. And it's not just that I saved a bunch of money on my car insurance!"

The audience's laughter breaks the tension, and the speaker continues. "The good news is that you are half-way on the road to everything you want. You already have the critical element necessary for success. When I asked how many of you held within you a burning desire, all of you raised your hands. Desire is the most important part of any achievement because it is within desire that success is born."

The speaker pauses to let the audience absorb the moment. Then, amazingly, he seems to stare right into Louis' eyes.

"Everyone desires something better for themselves," the speaker explains. "Have you ever wondered why so few seem to attain it? It's because most people are waiting for what they want to find them. Most fail to take their desire to the next level. In order to see the future you long for, you must create a personal vision, commit it to writing and act upon it." The speaker walks across the stage and makes a strong gesture to emphasize his point. "Are you listening?" he asks. "If you are, you now know why I was able to assure those 20 people that they will realize what they desire.

"Consider this," the speaker says. "If you can show me exactly where you want to go, I can tell you exactly how to get there. But if you cannot tell me where your journey will end, the best I can tell you is to simply start walking and wish you good luck.

"So have you decided?" the speaker asks. "Have I come here to speak only to you? Are you willing to take the next step that will begin to separate you from the crowd?"

Yvonne knew the answer. This time, Louis was squeezing her arm.

~~~~~

Why we act the way we do is based on a very simple principle: People either take the path of least resistance or do what's in their own self-interest. For many people, both of these motivations add up to simply getting through another day and doing what they have to do to make ends meet at the moment. For others, instant gratification and pursuing self-interest mean keeping up with the pace of those around them. Either way creates an endless cycle of chasing approval and acting according to the opinions of others.

The power of these outside forces vanishes, however, when you act in self-interest that is more than just getting through the day or pleasing others. When your actions are in support of self-interest based on a positive personal vision, every action produces a feeling of accomplishment. *Your actions pull your goal closer as you move toward it.* You are optimizing!

Most of us don't have a lot of time for reflection because we're always trying to figure out our next move. We navigate through life much like

> TRAVEL LOG TIP:
> Over the past 30 years, I have built four successful businesses—and I had to work very hard to do it. I had a husband, four children, friends and organization commitments. There were tough decisions to make, and I had to set priorities so that I could balance my time between business and personal responsibilities. Each business was a stepping-stone to the next. They started out small and grew into larger organizations requiring more commitment and creating larger burdens. But as they grew, I learned the importance of time management and maintaining a steady belief in my ideas. It was and still is a continuous process that takes time and energy. Being flexible during the process of life is important.
>
> *Ellyn*

we drive through a busy city. In the confusion of fast-paced living, success is defined as "getting there first," even when it's not really where you want to go! The pressure of life's pace often pushes us forward without enough information to support our actions. We get a few facts, make some assumptions, jump to a conclusion and stick with it no matter what.

In the mad dash to get there first—to know more, do more, have more, be more—it's only natural to look for shortcuts. But when you make snap judgments, you cheat yourself out of the rich experience of critical thinking, learning and growing. *Like concentrating only on the car in front of you on the highway during rush hour, ignoring your environment will only lead you into trouble.* Many accidents are caused by not paying attention to

> **TRAVEL LOG TIP:**
> *I have done more than 3,500 seminars and workshops based on creating change and harnessing the dynamics of action. I've discovered that it doesn't matter who is in the audience. At every workshop, people have an epiphany when they discover it's all pretty simple. Study any successful person at any level of achievement, and you'll discover the common ground of their achievement rests in four simple things:*
> - *Have an open mind,*
> - *Share the load,*
> - *Be willing to take a risk*
> - *Most important of all, take definite and necessary action.*
>
> *Ken*

what's happening around you. The basic principle of education is that you learn by building on what you already know. In other words, you need to pay attention to the signs along the way—one mile at a time.

Everyone processes information differently. So called left-brainers tend to want all the facts. Right-brainers generally can't be bothered with that degree of detail. They think in terms of concepts. Both types of people reach their destinations in different ways. Some will use a map loaded with details, while others follow their hunches—some people do a little bit of both. Which is right and which is wrong? If you get where you're going, it doesn't matter.

Regardless of your approach, draw yourself a map that will work for you. *People who stay focused on their destination despite the rat race around them end up with results they seek.* Whether the task is learning a new trade, getting a degree, writing a book or finding a sense of inner peace, true success is built slowly over time, with each mile traveled forward resulting in a positive change.

K.I.S.S.

Keep It Simple, Sweetie! Make a plan and make it doable. If your plan is too complicated, it may look good on paper, but when challenged by a lack of commitment, it's sure to fall apart. You won't enjoy the journey and you won't stay committed—and neither will those who support you. It is important to understand not only what you want to do in the future but also what you can do today. Continuous evaluation of where you are and what you have accomplished is key. Don't over-schedule or over-commit—but do commit yourself to live every day to the fullest in pursuit of your dream.

We all have choices—choices that can move us forward and choices that can hold us back and keep us unfulfilled. *Give yourself permission to make the choices that optimize your journey and propel you forward.* Eliminate things that eat away at your time and keep you from reaching your goals. All of us encounter "road signs" along the way—some call them circumstance or luck, even providence. We have to be aware enough to notice them, read them and heed them by making the course corrections they suggest.

Most important of all, make your plan actionable. Most people stop pursuing their dreams because their goal is too overwhelmingly big to take on—along with everything else in life. The answer to this problem seems obvious, doesn't it? Make the goal smaller. Break it down into more manageable pieces, and then take on those pieces one at a time. For example, while striving for world peace is a noble goal, getting along with your family is a great place to start. What can you get done in a week? A month? A year? (We'll talk more about exactly how to do this in the next section, "Act.")

Caution! Your Legacy Is Showing!

Your decisions and actions not only affect the people around you, they also determine your legacy. Will you be remembered as someone who tried to help others? You can share your time and your talent with others, and you can share your money. But that's not all: *Think of giving your attitude as a simple way of giving your energy to someone else through a smile or a listening ear, a pleasant hello, or a friendly comment to a service person.*

In today's "me first" culture, sharing your attitude is the kind of purposeful gift that is both powerful and priceless. Imagine that everyone's body is a mirror in which his or her actions and reactions are reflected. Then take it one step further and imagine those mirrors not only reflecting but also absorbing.

Of course, a mirror can only imitate, but as human beings we can initiate. Newton's third law of motion states that for every action there is a *re*action.

TRAVEL LOG TIP:
If life has taught me anything, it's that if you are not looking toward the future, you will stay mired in the present. You might think the present is just fine and dandy; most people who live in "the now" want to keep things as they are. But nothing ever stays the same. No good businessperson, for example, would be foolish enough to be satisfied with the present. Success means improving services and products, increasing revenues, training employees better. There is a lesson here for our personal lives. We must always be looking forward. Staying focused on the future provides us with a path to experience new situations, new opportunities and new people—a path to grow. *Ellyn*

NOTES:

In fact, the decisions you make today—even one as simple as committing yourself to share your positive energy with others—will produce results you can't begin to understand at the moment.

Consider the decisions your parents made and how they affected you. You are their legacy. *How you choose to live your life on a day-to-day basis will shape your legacy.* And your legacy will inevitably impact others. In Mitch Albom's book *The Five People You Meet in Heaven*, the main character, Eddie, learns how his life affected those around him. In the end he realizes "that each affects the other and the other affects the next, and the world is full of stories, but the stories are all one."[9]

TRAVEL PLANNING
What's your itinerary?

If you could accomplish any three goals this year, what would they be?_____

_____

_____

_____

Prioritize those goals. Which one would move you closer to achieving your dream? _____

_____

_____

List the shortcuts you have taken when you wished you had gone the distance.

_____

_____

_____

Celebrate your success. What projects or goals have you advanced in the last month? _____

_____

_____

Who are the most influential people in your life?_____

_____

_____

_____

If you could select anyone to guide you in your life, who would that be?_____

_____

_____

_____

What characteristics do they possess that make them a preferred guide? _____

_____

_____

_____

_____

Whose life or lives do you influence and is that meaningful to you? _____

_____

_____

_____

_____

Think of four people who are important to you. Would you be comfortable enough to ask them for a candid opinion of you? Or would you be anxious about their response? _____

_____

_____

_____

_____

_____

_____

What would be some small, simple things you could do if you wanted to change their impression of you? _____

_____

_____

_____

_____

_____

_____

Enter Here

You have traveled about half way along the Live Like You Mean It R.O.A.D. Take a moment to write down some thoughts about your journey so far. What do you want your future to look like? Are you ready to take some action toward accomplishing that dream?

_____

_____

_____

_____

_____

_____

_____

_____

_____

_____

_____

_____

_____

_____

_____

_____

R
O
A = ACT
D

Section 3

"Life is what we make it, always has been, always will be."
—Grandma Moses, artist

Go for It!

 There's No Turning Back.

 Be Careful!

 Bright Idea!

 Pause and Consider.

 Stop!

 Turn It Around.

On Your Way

Entering a Construction Zone

As the meeting starts, team members can't understand why Paul seems so angry. Watching him fidgeting in his chair, they know that he has something on his mind.

Joanne is at the front of the room, reviewing the results of the company's last campaign. She comments that although the numbers are reasonable, overall the promotion didn't do as well as anticipated and certainly could not be considered a success.

Paul sighs as he thinks about the words Joanne had used when she reviewed his job performance. "Here we go again," he muses, "another edition of the blame game."

Joanne continues, "C'mon people, this is—what?—the fourth mediocre campaign we've put together? What's going on? Are the prizes not big enough? Why can't you figure out what the salespeople want? I can remember—and it wasn't that long ago—when our promotions were so anticipated that competitors would lay low during that time because they knew we were out there capturing business. Now look at these results. It's going to be hard enough approaching Mr. B with lackluster results again, but when he sees the money we spent this time, he's going to hit the roof. I need some answers."

After a bit of a silence, Jeff offers, "I've heard from the sales force that the promotions run too long. They can't get excited about something that runs almost four months."

Courtney adds, "Yeah, I have heard that, too, but I also get the feeling from them that we put too many items on special at the same time."

"The technology is killing us," Steve chimes in. "Each salesperson has the ability to track his or her progress at the end of every week. I think the ones that are far behind the leaders just punch out and lose interest."

"In my opinion, we don't put items out there that people can get excited about anymore," Rick says. "I mean, you know how we used to run these things. We knew customers would be interested in special items at certain times of the year so we'd put them on promo then. The customers were excited we had the items they needed, and the salespeople were excited for the same reason. Now we study profitability charts and promote slow-moving items or items we can make more money on. We're not doing it for the customer anymore, and the salespeople know that."

Joanne jumps back in, "You know, I hear this kind of thing from you all the time. We don't do this right, and we don't do that right. If we listened to what the salespeople say, we'd have to: one, discount our most popular selling items; two, raise commission rates; three, have week-long promos; and four, get off their backs. Haven't we heard all of this before?" she continues. "These are just excuses for poor performance, and I am tired of dealing with the symptoms. I want to know what the root of our problem is. Can any of you tell me something that I haven't heard before? Paul, you haven't said anything yet."

And he hadn't planned to say anything.

"So Paul, any thoughts?" Joanne asks.

"All right," Paul says, "I'll give you my opinion. I think the promotions we develop are fine. They push the items we need pushed, and they raise brand awareness. The problem isn't with the promotions. That's why every time we change a promotion, the results are the same. Our situation is what it is because of a roadblock at the next level. Think about it for a second. Who sits between every department in this company and our customers?"

"The salesperson," Courtney responds.

"Right," Paul says. "And while we have been asking the sales department to do more, so has everyone else. For example, over the past two years the tech group rolled out a new ordering system that the customers need to learn through our salespeople. Finance went on a new accounts receivable management program that has to be monitored and enforced by the salesperson. Logistics moved to an electronic catalog with a huge learning curve and sales added that self-directed product-pricing piece. Then, just two months ago, all the reps went through a GPS program to learn how to co-ordinate their own route delivery times."

"We know all this," Joanne says. "What's your point?"

"I'm saying," Paul replies, "that a salesperson is just that—a person. They have a finite amount of time, energy and capacity. And while all of these departments, including ours, have wonderful new goals, the reality is that we will see our goals realized only if the salesperson makes them happen."

Heads bobbing around in the room indicate consensus with Paul's reasoning.

"So is your suggestion that we pull back, Paul?" Joanne asks.

"No," he answers, "my suggestion is that we find ways to off-load our salespeople's activity. Look, we know these people love to sell—they love to compete—but this company has tied up their hands and feet with so many tasks. Sales reps should be hired to sell—period.

"Unfortunately," he continues, "selling has become just another function on a complicated list. We'll get our reps back in the game and direct more of their attention toward our goal if we make their lives easier. Let's take some responsibility for what's been happening and put an end to the blame game."

Team members broke out in applause of support for Paul's position.

And for once, Joanne was speechless.

~~~~~~

Sticking with the status quo might make life a lot easier, but learning, meeting challenges and growing make life worth living. We believe that three powerful tools—awareness, participation and contribution—can help you break away from the ordinary and navigate the road to your future.

Your Roadside Toolkit

"Be there or be square." That's what the Fonz used to say on *Happy Days*. And he was right: ***Awareness*** is where it's at! You beat most people just by showing up every day ready to go, alert and primed for action. Have you ever talked to a group about an exciting idea and have some of them blankly stare back at you? That's what happens when you're "there," but they aren't.

Being aware—knowing where you want to go *with your life—is critical to owning it and making it more meaningful and satisfying.* Many of us fill our days doing mindless stuff like moving papers into piles, reshuffling the piles, checking email and (admit it!) playing solitaire on the computer. This may be activity,

> TRAVEL LOG TIP:
> There are so many things in life that we feel are unimportant—not worth the time or commitment or just in the way. We push them aside or don't do them at all. But if you are like me, the things that you put off doing often turn out to be the situations where you learn something new, meet someone who becomes important in your life, or find an opportunity that is a turning point in your life. I try to remember that when I don't want to do something it might turn out to be the experience that opens the next door for me.　　　　　*Ellyn*
>
> NOTES:

but it's not progress. A "busy" schedule like that can leave little time for thinking and planning! But thinking and planning are exactly what you must do to put your best foot forward on the road to awareness.

It's no accident that awareness is the first step of any 12-step program.

In order to accomplish anything in life, the first thing you must do is show up and be present, well aware of your surroundings, what you desire and what you need to do to get it.

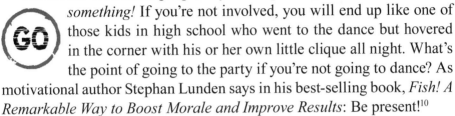

You'll beat even more people if you add **participation** to the mix: *Do something!* If you're not involved, you will end up like one of those kids in high school who went to the dance but hovered in the corner with his or her own little clique all night. What's the point of going to the party if you're not going to dance? As motivational author Stephan Lunden says in his best-selling book, *Fish! A Remarkable Way to Boost Morale and Improve Results*: Be present![10]

Acting on a commitment is what's important. Have you ever wondered, for example, why health clubs can afford to charge only $20 a month for annual membership? To them it's free money. If 50 people sign up and only one keeps going, they've made $11,760 for doing nothing. They're capitalizing on an unfortunate trait of human nature—the spirit is willing, but the flesh is weak. Indeed, the road to the health club—and many other commitments—is paved with good intentions. But it's participation that helps you get there. And that's how you understand the next rule of the road—*contribution.*

There is participating and there is PARTICIPATING. The amount of energy you contribute to an activity proportionately affects what you get out of that activity. Decisions such as

> TRAVEL LOG TIP:
> For years I made the excuse that I didn't have time to exercise. I was in the office 12+ hours a day and on the road 150+ days a year. How was I ever going to squeeze another hour into the day? I made a deal with myself: I would get up 45 minutes earlier than usual and go to work 30 minutes later. It worked. I have exercised faithfully for a year and a half. Before, I made excuses; now, I have made a commitment. I was determined. We can all find 30 minutes or an hour each day to do the things that are really important to us. Give up something to take something on that will really make a difference for you and how you live your life.   *Ellyn*
>
> NOTES:

writing a book, getting a new job, starting a new project, learning a foreign language or playing a musical instrument all take the same two things: determination and commitment. When you were a child, the adults around you held you accountable—do your homework, clean your room, practice the piano, etc. As an adult, you must do this for yourself. By holding yourself accountable and not relying on an outside authority to make the rules and enforce them, you move beyond participation to contribution.

Often, participators stop short of taking a risk. They wait for others to tell them what to do. Contributors, however, are willing to take risks by taking action—even if that action is to simply ask "What if?" At that moment, when you offer an idea—a part of yourself—you are contributing.

> **TRAVEL LOG TIP:**
> What we must do is identify each baby step that will get us and keep us on the path toward our goal. When I started my first business at the age of 22, I knew very little if anything about running a company—but that didn't stop me. I had a lot to learn, but I started small. All I knew when I started was that I wanted my own consulting company. That was my vision of point Z. Getting from here to there took 15 years—definitely not an overnight success, but a success nonetheless. Now, some 30 years after starting that first venture, I run an internationally recognized company. I won't say it has been easy, but it has been fun and fulfilling, and I did it one step at a time. Goals once accomplished simply evolve to a new and higher level. I am always trying to kick it up a notch.   *Ellyn*
>
> NOTES:

Your ability and willingness to invest yourself is why it is so important to select your activities carefully. Focus on and fully apply yourself to what moves you toward your goal. And with this in mind, remember that "doing something" can mean getting something *off* your list as much as it means adding something to it. It's like getting ready for a trip. Your to-do list may include packing, getting the car serviced, stopping the mail and newspaper and making reservations. Getting all this *off* your list is what pulls you toward your goal.

In section four, "Deliver," we will talk more about the long-term and less tangible rewards that come with dedicating yourself to your goal and living your life in a purposeful way.

Are We There Yet?

To make your dream a reality, it helps to picture yourself where you want to be. For example, as we suggested in section one, "Recognize," go to the car dealership and sit in the car of your dreams, or if you are just entering college, go to graduation ceremonies and picture yourself accepting your diploma. In other words, visualize the end result. Experience the moment in your mind over and over again. Make it real—but don't stop there. Make your dream actionable.

One of the most common reasons why many people don't reach their goals is that the goals are just too overwhelming, especially in light of everything else happening in their lives. So the trick is to make the goal more manageable by breaking it into pieces and tackling one piece at a time.

TRAVEL LOG TIP:
In the early 1990s, I was reading everything I could get my hands on about motivation. I heard about the "Yale Study of 1953." The story goes that in this study, the graduating class of '53 was asked a simple question: "How many of you have definitive personal and financial goals for your future and have developed a plan to achieve those goals?" Only 3 percent of the class said "yes." Many years later, Yale went back to the same people and determined their net worth. They discovered that each member of the 3 percent group was worth more than all members of the 97 percent group collectively. I immediately took this information to heart and became very serious about developing my goals and plans. Much later I discovered one big problem with the Yale study: It never really happened! It's just a story that's been traveling around the speakers' circuit and Internet for years. But that's okay with me. True story or not, it made me think twice about the importance of having goals and a plan to achieve them.   *Ken*

NOTES:

Most people look at their lives as the model below suggests. They are at point A now; they want to reach point B. To try to shorten the trip, some people will work harder, longer or faster, or they may even borrow money to pull the dream closer. Others won't have the drive or discipline to make any effort. Either way, when it doesn't work out the way they want, they just give up.

Let's look at point B differently. Let's call it your "end-state vision"—the place where you want to end up. The arrow that connects A to B is the process that you will need to go through to get there.

TRAVEL LOG TIP:
As you begin to give yourself permission to let go of your fears, you lighten your load and free yourself to move forward. The presentations I give today are far better than those I gave 20 or 30 years ago—even 10 years ago. I have watched other speakers, become more passionate about my messages, left behind some of my old techniques and learned new ones. If we are not continually enhancing and refining our personal skill set, we become stagnant. Keep trying new things! *Ken*

NOTES:

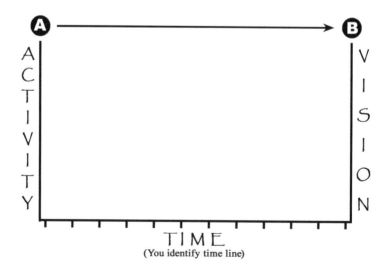

TIME
(You identify time line)

Now let's cross out B and change it to Z and then fill in 24 letters (B-Y) in between A and Z. In this way, Z becomes your end-state vision, and B through Y are the doable steps necessary to get there, arranged in a manageable, achievable order. (You may need fewer or more steps in your plan.)

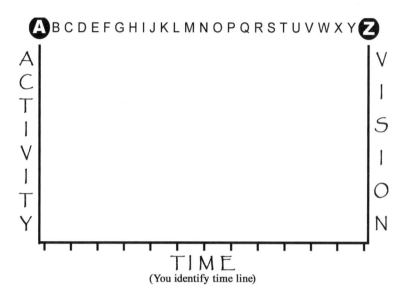

For starters, just do what is needed to get to point B. Don't worry about the other steps. Over the time it takes to reach your ultimate goal and depending upon the process you follow, you will be adding a new collection of skills to your mix while pulling your end-stage vision ever closer. For example, perhaps you have a longtime desire to change your career path: You are working in retail management now and would like to become a nurse. If you don't set up some intermediate goals between retail management and becoming a nurse, your motivation may fizzle out. Check out nursing sites on the Internet, contact nursing schools for information and talk to some nurses. Digging for information is how you will determine the steps you must take to get from where you are today to your end-stage vision: (Your name here), RN.

Move It... and Lose It

A very important yet easily overlooked aspect of this process is negotiating with yourself over what you are willing to sacrifice to achieve your goal. Each step may require giving something up in order to progress. (Remember "optimizing" from section two?) Be realistic about what you can do given your other responsibilities. To start, focus on taking steps that are most important and will move you forward quickly.

Just the act of getting started may be your point B. Ideally, by achieving that smaller goal and subsequent ones, you are not only pulling your end-stage vision closer but also giving up activities that bind you to the past.

Put the Pedal to the Metal

So why not start now? Enough with the excuses. Yes, the first step is often the hardest. An innate fear of the unknown may feel like a barricade—a "road closed" sign holding you back. Your gut response may be to shift to neutral and idle—that is, procrastinate. But all it really takes is getting in gear and tapping the gas to start building momentum.

Ultimately, how you choose to spend each day will determine what you accomplish in life. In the time it takes to rationalize why something can't be done, you might have it done twice over! All you really need is willingness and that comes from attitude. We'll talk more about fear, procrastination and the power of attitude in the next chapter.

TRAVEL PLANNING
Where do you go from here?

Do you need some expertise to get where you want to go? List options._____

_____

_____

_____

_____

Do you know anyone who can help you? Who? _____

_____

_____

_____

Are there some areas you need to work on?

_____ Appearance   _____Networking

_____ Wardrobe   _____Equipment

_____ Attitude   _____Classes

_____ Resume   _____Internet research

Briefly explain._____

_____

_____

Are you willing to take some risks to get where you want to go? Why? _____

_____

_____

_____

_____

_____

Can you break your goal down into smaller, achievable pieces that are more manageable? List smaller goals. _____

_____

_____

_____

_____

_____

_____

_____

_____

What are the most important things you can do now to move forward? Remember that "doing" can mean adding or removing something from your life.___

_____

_____

_____

_____

_____

_____

_____

_____

_____

_____

_____

_____

_____

_____

R
O
A= ACT
D

8

Roadblocks and Detours
The Long and Winding Road

Walking through the terminal, Dave thinks about how the sky and warm temperatures make the day an excellent one for flying.

And that's a good thing, because no matter how often he flies for his job, air travel is one of those things that seems unnatural to him. He smiles as he thinks about how his father's laundry list of excuses not to fly probably planted the idea in his head.

"If man had been meant to fly, he would have been born with wings," his father would say every time Dave or his brothers or sisters tried to talk him into flying instead of driving. Dave, the youngest one in the family, learned by watching the older kids, not to argue with his father about flying, especially, when he witnessed the argument that ensued when his brother Mike said, "C'mon dad, if man had been meant to ride 60 miles an hour down the highway, he would have been born with wheels instead of feet and would have a 400 horse engine on his back. So what's the difference? A car. A plane. They're both just machines."

Thinking about how a plane is just a machine doesn't make flying any easier today, despite the nice weather. Now settled in his seat, Dave flips through a magazine and tries to get his mind off the flight until they are off the ground and in the air. Looking around, Dave notices the cabin is only half full. When the flight attendant closes the door, he puts the magazine into the seat-back pocket, sits back and closes his eyes. As he tries to relax, Dave can't help overhearing the conversation between two men seated behind him. It isn't long before Dave finds himself listening with interest to their exchange.

The older of the two men is heading to California to visit with his son's family. The younger man is on the road to sell. It isn't long before the men's cordial exchange deepens with the salesman talking about his life and the other man listening and periodically responding with a comment or two. Then the younger man asks, "So if you had to do it all over again, what would you change?"

The older man asks a question in return, "Did you ever hear that poem the Red Hat Ladies use? When my wife was healthier, she was a red-hatter. She used to love to get together with her girlfriends. They'd wear their big red hats as crowns, laugh and have the most wonderful times. Whenever they had a meeting, they would recite the poem, 'When I Am an Old Woman I Shall Wear Purple.' "

"Anyway," the older man continues, "my wife used to come home and tell me she wished she'd had that much fun when she was young. I was happy that she was enjoying herself, but I never really understood her need for it. I had always been content staying clear of change."

The young man quickly chimes in, "So what are your three greatest accomplishments in life?"

"Well, I don't know about three," the older man says, "but I can tell you what my number one accomplishment is."

"OK, then, what's that?" the younger man asks.

"It happened about 10 years ago," the older man explains, "when I decided to stop thinking and fearing and start living. That's why I'm on this plane. I'm overcoming my fears and visiting my kids. I know my wife would be proud of me. I take her with me wherever I go. She's the voice in my head and the best of my heart. Her passing lead to my awakening."

Dave's heart sinks as he wipes away a lone tear running down his cheek. The plane jerks and he can feel the wheels running across the black tar of the runway. He glances back at the young man, wondering if he has been equally touched by the story, but he is already gone. The old man catches his eye and smiles. Words are not needed. Dave has received the message and will take it with him.

~~~~~

Obstacles in the road—we face them every day. Carefully maneuvering around pylons and learning from experience— both positive and negative—are what keep us on track. Life happens, and when you really want to succeed, you find a way over, around or through the challenges thrown in your path. Maybe it involves asking others for help, rethinking priorities, or trying a different path or maybe a whole new direction. Occasional tweaks to the plan are not only necessary, they are essential—as long as they are done in the context of achieving your goal.

There are no shortcuts *or easy ways out when you really want to succeed.* The secret is having a can-do attitude that's bigger and stronger than the fear and procrastination that may threaten to impede your progress.

> TRAVEL LOG TIP:
> When my son was 7 years old, we lived near a large park with a sandpit that had a long rope hanging over it. The kids would climb a pile of railroad ties, grab the rope, swing into the pit and drop into the sand. Every time we went to the park, my son would watch the other kids do this, but I could never get him to try it. Then one day, he wanted me to take him to the park in the rain. He was insistent, so I did. When we arrived, not another soul was in sight. He climbed the pile of railroad ties, grabbed the rope and sailed to the middle of the pit. He got up and did it again. "OK, Mom," he said. "We can go home now. I wanted to be sure I wouldn't fall off the rope." In other words, he needed to build some confidence so he would not look like a failure in front of the other kids.   *Ellyn*
>
> NOTES:

Later, Later, Later

Procrastination is a trait many of us must deal with daily, but most of us postpone until tomorrow. When something is too complicated, takes too much time to do or isn't fun, we put it off. Some things—like postponing cleaning the closet or washing the car—have no detrimental effect on your life. But when you procrastinate on getting started on your goals, that's a different story. You know you are avoiding something when:

- It's been on your "to do" list for a year.
- You get angry just thinking about it.
- You can't motivate yourself to get the information you need to complete the project.
- You lose the information you need.
- You talk about it all the time but don't do it.
- Everything you see reminds you of it—also known as the "nagging at me" syndrome.

A common reason for procrastination is lack of confidence—feeling like you don't have enough knowledge or information to proceed. As Joel Barker, author of *Future Edge: Discovering the New Paradigms for Success* (and many other motivational books), notes, if you wait for enough information before you act on your idea, you'll have to accept the fact that you'll never have enough.[11] *Real success demands that you get started—somewhere, anywhere!—with an open mind and a willingness to take risks.*

> TRAVEL LOG TIP:
> I had a friend who was in a corporate position at a Fortune 500 foodservice company. In the early 1990s, she began having severe health problems, which ultimately developed into multiple sclerosis. As the years went on, although her arms and legs became lifeless, she never stopped doing. When all she had left was her weakened voice and her brain power, we set up a computer with voice-recognition software. She started a newsletter and chatroom on the Internet for other MS victims. She had a good reason to just quit, but she never did. She forged ahead using her communications skills to help others.   *Ellyn*
>
> NOTES:

Remember: You can't retrieve time lost to procrastination. You and you alone are accountable for that time. Don't wake up 10 or 20 years from now with regrets because of excuses you made today. Do you appreciate a beautiful sunset? How many have you seen? Do you find peace and tranquility gazing at a waterfall? How many have you sought out? Do you like to go fishing—maybe it brings back warm childhood memories? How often do you cast a line? What separates the doers from the procrastinators is their refusal to avoid opportunity. Achievers take action.

Drive Through the Fear

We all have fears, and each of us has built a shell around ourselves to protect us from those fears. Like driving a car with no windows, we're moving but can't see where we're going. Trying so hard to protect ourselves, we often lose our vision. The first step toward conquering a fear is recognizing that it exists. Do you have an old script you need to shelve? Are you still following someone else's map for your life? Did your parents or teachers put you down? *Do you still remember hearing what you couldn't*

TRAVEL LOG TIP:
There was a time in my life when my greatest fear was public speaking. As a child, I was frightened to read aloud in class and I could never give a speech or participate in a debate. Every summer, I would volunteer to work on a play given by the junior theater. I chose to work on costumes and sets because I was afraid of being on the other side of the curtain. Now I realize that I missed out on a lot of great opportunities. Since then, I have attacked my fear of public speaking ferociously. In my late 20s, I was asked to speak at a professional meeting and accepted. I carefully wrote out every word. As I approached the podium, my palms were sweaty and my knees were shaking. I grabbed onto either side of the podium with a death grip! Several minutes into the experience, I realized I wasn't reading my speech; I was talking to an audience of colleagues. Now, 30 years later, I have given hundreds of presentations. That is not to say I don't get butterflies in my stomach and feel my heart pounding. But that adrenaline rush gives me the boost I need to get started. And I know that if I set my mind to something, I can do it. Ellyn

do? Never mind all that. The only person you have to prove anything to is yourself. Take the challenge and conquer your fear.

Fear of making the wrong decision can result in your making no decision at all. Those "what if" fears can be paralyzing. But when a decision does not involve life or death, and when it doesn't hurt another person, it shouldn't be hard to make. No one expects perfection right out of the chute. Learning to accept "baby-step" accomplishments is important. Remember steps A to Z? In fact, the best way to learn something is to *not* be successful at it the first time around. Analyze what went wrong, chat with colleagues or friends for some insight on new options, then make a mid-course correction. Remember: Thomas Edison invented the electric light bulb after 1000 attempts! But each attempt brought him closer to where he wanted to be.

Life is a continuous journey of exploration. The more you explore, the more you discover, understand and enhance your journey. *The simple act of doing something is an act of learning.* Whether you surprise yourself with what you already know or discover how much you still must learn, you win! The more you learn, the more secure you become in decision-making—and come to realize that most of your worrying is about things that will never happen!

TRAVEL PLANNING
Do it NOW!

Are you willing to be honest with yourself? If not, why? _____

_____

_____

_____

_____

_____

_____

What is stopping you from taking the action you want to take? Explain. _____

_____

_____

_____

_____

_____

_____

What decisions have you been putting off that need to be made now? _____

_____

_____

_____

_____

_____

_____

_____

What keeps you from acting? _____

_____

_____

_____

_____

_____

_____

What detours in life have been positive for you? _____

_____

_____

_____

_____

_____

_____

What detours have taken you off track and away from your goal? _____

_____

_____

_____

_____

_____

_____

_____

_____

Rough Road Ahead

Dodging the Potholes

High school reunions are often predictable. Five years is the first landmark. Classmates are still pretty close to one another, and the memories of the past remain fresh. At age 23, most are either getting close to or just getting out of college, and even those who chose another path aren't feeling quite settled. There are few marriages and even fewer children.

At the 10-year mark, the culling begins. Fewer people show up for the party, and a competition for status sets the tone. College and grad school are over, careers are underway and many people are married. Conversations seem to revolve around money, cars, trips and other things that are supposed to symbolize success.

The 15-year party is where the great divide happens. People congregate into the "cliques" that were so prevalent "back in the day." The men head to a corner of the room while the women reunite at the 8-foot tables.

Tom has three memories of his 15-year reunion: how people who continued to socialize after graduation stuck together; how hard it was to break into any established group; and how even though the gathering was billed as a dance, few took to the dance floor but rather hid now "mature" figures by remaining seated. Tom left early that evening, explaining to his wife that he couldn't believe how some things never change.

It was after the 15th reunion that Tom decided he wouldn't attend any more of the pointless gatherings. He was stung by both the bragging and the judgments. The staple of every conversation was "and so what do you do?" The fact that Tom didn't quite have the career part of his life figured out yet brought out a few of what he calls "BMW stares," where a person pulls the top of his head back a little so you see his nose like the "nostrils" on the front of the luxury car. As more and more time passed, high school became a faded memory.

Then one day, Tom receives a voicemail at the office from a fellow who introduces himself as Mark Kelly. "Tommy," he says, "it's been over 30 years since we were in high school together. I'd love to see you, so let me know when I can drop by your office."

Tom remembers Mark as being a good friend throughout their high school years, and he is grateful for that. Tom was a heavyset nerd back then, but Mark was one of those people others noticed and listened to. Tom was glad they were friends because knowing Mark gave him a kind of limited entry into the popular groups. He quickly returns Mark's call, leaving the message, "This Thursday at noon for lunch would be great."

Tom figures that at this stage in life, Mark probably wants to see him for one of two reasons. Either he has something to sell him, or he needs help. "Either way," Tom thinks, "I should find out what I can do for him, and it'll be great to see him again and catch up."

On Tuesday, Tom's office phone rings right before noon and the receptionist, Kay, says, "Someone who says he is your high school friend is in the lobby."

Tom nervously puts on his sport coat and heads down the stairs. In the lobby, amidst all the suits, sits a fellow sporting a scruffy beard and wearing a flannel shirt and jeans.

"Mark? Mark Kelly?" Tom asks.

Sure enough, the man rises and an unmistakable smile comes over his face as he holds his hand outstretched. Still physically fit, he is shorter than Tom remembered—way shorter.

"Tommy, you jerk," says Mark. "You never come to reunions anymore. What's the matter? Too good for the rest of us now?"

The comment takes Tom aback, but he laughs it off with some excuse and suggests they head out to lunch.

"So, Mark, tell me about your life," Tom begins.

"Oh, the typical stuff," Mark replies. "A couple of bad marriages, couple of kids. I'm single now. My sister is letting me live in her basement while I go through this latest divorce, so I have enough money to make my child support payments."

After listening for a few minutes, Tom decides to change the subject and asks if Mark still sees any of their old high school classmates.

Mark begins with a recap of the recent 30-year reunion and the years since graduation—which women flirted with him and which guys had receding hairlines. He mentions some who have died and some who just never change. Tom listens cordially but soon realizes that this person, whose opinion he had once valued so highly, is still living in his "glory days." As the conversation continues, Tom finds himself daydreaming, thinking about how funny it is that most of the people whose opinions he valued back then really don't matter to him anymore.

He interrupts a story about how in 11th grade Mark had dropped his girlfriend off at midnight and then had gone out with a different girl, and Tom asks, "Mark, there has to be some reason you called me after all these years out of the blue. What can I do for you?"

Mark's face tightens up. He begins by mentioning that he is starting a business marketing personalized trinkets and "trash" items for promotions and how he is hoping the company Tom works for might be able to help him with an order.

Tom explains that all of that business is handled contractually through another department but that he will be glad to pass a business card and recommendation along. That being said, the conversation comes to an end, and Tom pays the lunch tab.

Driving back to work, Tom considers how during the past 90 minutes, Mark never once asked a question about him, his family, his interests or his professional life. As he parks his car and walks back into the building, he considers how many times in his life he has been influenced by the opinion of people he thought knew better, and how many times he had been disappointed by the result.

"That mistake probably happens to everyone," he reasons. "After all, you have to listen to the opinions of others until you reach a point where you can tell the difference between those who want to keep you right where you are and those who support what they see you can become."

He hopes that he has become the latter type.

"Good afternoon, Tom," the receptionist greets him. "Did you have a nice lunch?"

"Yes, I did, Kay," he replies. "Thanks for asking."

"Did you have fun reminiscing?" Kay wonders.

"Actually, Kay, it was thinking about the past that reminded me how good it feels to be right here in the present," Tom happily replies.

~~~~~~

While it always helps to have other people on your team, it's not always possible to count on that support. *Your best source of positive energy is always yourself.* When you truly believe in what you are trying to accomplish, that belief becomes a spark plug that keeps the passion burning.

No Bad Attitudes Allowed

How we approach any situation affects the outcome. If you allow your emotions to get the best of you, you may not get the response you are seeking. Attitude is everything. *You have the ability to stop negative emotions from interfering with your ability to handle a difficult situation or respond to an opportunity.*

Everyone loves to be around people who are motivated, optimistic, upbeat, warm and caring—people who see their gas tank as half full rather than half empty. Many successful people are said to have this kind of charisma. They are comfortable with themselves, and their energy and enthusiasm are like magnets that attract us to them and inspire us.

> TRAVEL LOG TIP:
> When I need a motivational reminder about action, all I have to do is look out the window as I am driving down the street. There seems to be a Subway franchise on every corner. Talk about a great idea! Really, it's just a sandwich, but look what one guy did with it! There really are no original ideas flying around the cosmos waiting for someone to snare them. Every idea comes from something we see, hear or experience. "New" ideas are built from something or someone else's input and foundation. The more we do, hear, read and experience, the more creative resources we have.   *Ken*
>
> NOTES:

You can make the decision every day to be this kind of person. You can wake up looking forward to the beginning of the day or dreading what lies ahead. The choice is yours. All of us have the ability to be positive and emote "good vibes." Even when you encounter negative people, you can energize them with a positive attitude. *If you can't turn around a negative person, move on before they bring you down, too.*

On the other hand, a positive attitude breeds positive action and interaction. Have you ever found yourself thinking that some people have all the luck? Guess what? It's not luck. It's attitude. An upbeat, positive person always attracts the "lucky" opportunity, like meeting the right people and having the right situation fall into his or her lap. On the other hand, negativism repels opportunity. After all, with whom would you rather spend five minutes—a positive person or a negative one? Would you rather be around a happy person or someone who goes through life whining and complaining?

TRAVEL LOG TIP:
I have always been the kind of person who wants to make a decision and get it over with. I know I can be very impatient. I don't like details and tend to live by my gut feelings. I get just enough facts to say "yes" and then six months down the road, when more is revealed, I realize that making that snap judgment didn't necessarily take me where I wanted to go. It has only been in the past few years that I have learned how to slow down, go with the flow and gather a few more facts before I jump in. Life is so pressured that we feel we have to make decisions instantaneously, but few decisions need to be made that quickly.   *Ellyn*

NOTES:

Very few of us have lived a perfect life. All of us have encountered difficult people, situations and experiences (notice we did not say "failures"). No matter how many challenges or difficulties you have faced over the years, the only way to truly change your life is to change your attitude today, tomorrow, the next day and the day after that. Follow these steps to a positive attitude every day:

1. Get up on the "right side of the bed."
2. Do one thing that will move you closer to your goal, even if you spend only 10 minutes at the beginning of the day doing so.
3. Give yourself some "think time" every day.
4. Keep smiling.
5. Do something nice for someone when he/she least expects it, even if it's just giving a compliment.
6. Turn negative thoughts into positive opportunities.
7. Become a positive magnet. Repel the negative.
8. Don't raise your voice. Speak with kindness.
9. Take a risk. Do something new or different.
10. BELIEVE YOU CAN!

Beware of Backseat Drivers

Once you declare your intention to act on your dream, the strength of that declaration becomes attractive to some—and repulsive to others. No matter what those naysaying backseat drivers say or do, remember *you* are the one behind the wheel. No excuses. If others can't see and share your dream, move on. This is not to say that discussion and exploration of other ideas are not useful. Constructive criticism can be valuable, but in the last analysis, you choose your destination and you choose how you are going to get there.

TRAVEL LOG TIP:
Every day I find myself inspired by those around me, by hearing their stories, appreciating their accomplishments, and watching them grow and evolve. Even if nothing else happens, each day we can expect to be surrounded by information and stimulation that inspires us. Even standing in line at the bank or at an amusement park or in an office building elevator, we are constantly being educated, entertained and stimulated. Just when I think I am so overworked and stressed out that I can't do one more thing, I will hear a story that inspires me to push ahead.   *Ellyn*

NOTES:

Maybe the first, the second or even the third route you select won't be

perfect, but you'll learn from every attempt.

The more you believe in yourself, the stronger your self-esteem becomes. The stronger your self-esteem, the better able you'll be to sift through the advice and opinions of others and select the ideas that are most meaningful and helpful to you. Sharing your journey with people who are constructive in their comments is extremely important. These are the people who understand *success is a process.* Harness their energy to help you move toward your dream. Motivators encourage you to push your limits. They find ways to work around any obstacles. Criticizers come and go, but those who inspire us, mentor us and move us to a higher level, stay with us always.

TRAVEL LOG TIP:
Some say I am the eternal optimist. If I really believe in something and really want to do it, no one can stop me. But I didn't always have the self-confidence I have today. Taking small risks and trying new things made me who I am today. I don't sit on the sidelines and watch those around me continue to do things the same old way. For everything, there is always another, maybe better, way. But you never find it unless you try. Successful people are always looking for a new way; everybody else is satisfied with the status quo.   Ellyn

NOTES:

TRAVEL PLANNING
Time to tune up your attitude!

What attitudes do you feel hold you back from achieving your goals?

_____ *Other people have all the luck.*

_____ *You were born to the wrong parents.*

_____ *You are not as smart as other people.*

_____ *You never get a break.*

_____ *You don't have any time.*

_____ *You carry too many personal burdens.*

_____ *You are not well educated.*

What can you do to turn these negatives into positives? _____

_____

_____

What choices are you willing to make every day to bring you closer to accomplishing your goals? _____

_____

_____

_____

How can you find 30–60 minutes several times a week to work on achieving your goals? _____

_____

_____

ROAD= DELIVER

Section 4

"Memories of our lives, our works and our deeds
will continue in others."

—Rosa Parks, civil rights activist

Go for It!

 There's No Turning Back.

 Be Careful!

 Bright Idea!

 Pause and Consider.

 Stop!

 Turn It Around.

Cresting the Hill

What's Your ETA?

"Hi, Dad!" says J.J.

"Hi, J.J.," his father replies. "Is everything okay?"

"Yeah, I just need to talk to you," J.J. explains. "Got a minute?"

"Always, for you," his father says. "What's up with my soon-to-be college graduate?"

"I'm just getting a little frustrated," J.J. says, "and need to talk with somebody."

"I'm glad you called," J.J.'s father says. "To tell you the truth, I've been missing the little phone chats we used to have over the years. Remember? They started when you were in grade school. I always knew I could expect a call about 3:30 when school got out. Lately, I've been missing those days."

"Oh," J.J. says sheepishly, "sorry about that. I have good intentions, but there always seems to be one more thing that needs doing. Next thing I know, it's too late. There are never enough hours in the day."

"Well," J.J.'s father says, "you can see the end in sight now, so take some consolation in that."

"I don't know, Dad," J.J. explains. "I'm starting to think the pressure's never going to end. Now my friends are talking about interviews, graduate school and getting married."

"That shouldn't bother you," his father suggests. "Everyone's just looking forward to graduation and the next step."

"Not everybody, Dad," J.J. says. "I guess that's why I'm calling."

"So what's up?" his father asks. "Trouble in school?"

"No, no nothing like that," J.J. assures his father. "I'm going to graduate on time. It's just that I've been so focused on getting this degree that

I never really had time to think about what comes next. And now there is all this pressure—from everyone."

"Am I talking to the same person who usually never listens to anybody?" J.J.'s father asks.

"It's just that I'm starting to wonder if I'm doing it all the right way," J.J. confesses.

"Truthfully, it started in grade school—everyone asking questions. Are you going to join scouts? Are you going to play a sport? What do you want to be when you grow up? In high school, the questions started to change: Who are you going out with? What clubs are you joining? What college are you going to go to? What are you going to study?"

"Well," J.J.'s father says, "you can't be upset that people were curious about what you wanted to do with your life, can you? People are curious, and they ask because they care about you."

"I wonder about that," J.J. says.

"You wonder if we care about you?" J.J.'s father asks. "C'mon, you can't be serious. What's this really all about?"

"Dad, think about it," says J.J. "All my life, people have wanted to know what I'm going to do next. It's like they weren't happy with what I was. It was always what I was going to do next that mattered most. And now ... "

"And now," J.J.'s father interrupts, "you don't have a next?"

"Yeah," J.J. replies, "I just don't know what's going to happen."

"You'll figure it out. I've got faith in you," his father assures J.J. "Right now, it's okay to take a deep breath and enjoy how far you've come. Do you know how few people in our family have gone to college?"

"It's just frustrating to be at this point and to be confused," J.J. admits.

"I completely understand," his father says. "I remember when your mother and I wanted to get married, and there was such an age differ-ence between us. Seven years doesn't seem like a lot now, but back then, everyone was challenging us on it. All we wanted to do was get married. When the day finally came and we were driving off to our honeymoon, we realized that we hadn't made a lot of plans beyond that.

"And now look at us," he continues, "we've been married for 30 years and have you and your sisters. It's been great, but it took time to figure out what we wanted for our future. We didn't make all the decisions at once; rather, we made them one at a time. Whatever you want for yourself, con-sider the alternatives, pick one and start going for it."

"So what you're saying, Dad, is that working toward a goal, making it happen and then getting a new goal is a process that lasts forever?" J.J. asks.

"Well, it may not happen the same way for everyone," his father replies. "I wouldn't say that's true for everyone, but I will tell you this: The people who feel lost as they go through life are usually the ones who let others affect their decisions. I know you. You're not one of those people. Don't be overly concerned that you haven't figured out your next step. Enjoy where you are right now."

"Thanks, Dad," J.J. says. "I feel a whole lot better. Love you!"

"Hey, I have just one question," his Dad says. "The next time someone asks you what your next step is, what are you going to say?"

"That I have no idea, but I'll let them know when I get there," J.J. happily replies.

~~~~~

"**A**re we there yet?" If you're a parent, you've probably heard little voices from the back seat asking this question—repeatedly. It's a question you'll be asking, too, as you travel the road toward accomplishing your goals: Am I there yet? And how will I *know* when I am?

The good news is that until you take your final breath you are never "there," because new goals and new challenges are always on the horizon. You will discover that as fulfilling as

cresting the hill can be, the real thrill lies in seeing new possibilities—the stuff of new dreams—unfold before you. *That's when the real question becomes not "Am I there yet?" but rather, "Where can I go from here?"*

Imagine you have had your sights set on becoming a chemist. You have gone to college and graduate school, going through the process of semester after semester, class after class, project after project, one day at a time as your goal comes into view. The fact is, however, more than half of college students change their major at least once, and according to the U.S. Department of Labor, the average college graduate changes jobs once every three years and changes career fields two or three times over a lifetime.[12,13] In other words, as you get closer to your goal, you may find it changing into something new. Life is a constantly changing and evolving process—and it's also a learning process. With more information and more passion, you may choose to tweak or even redirect your goal. When you reach the top of the mountain, you might want to take a side road and see a new perspective.

What's Next?

There are many definitions of success—financial, intellectual, emotional, social. You can be successful in one, some or all of these areas. Most of us define success according to what we see in others. Earlier we talked about getting caught up in the "gottas"—gotta have this, gotta have that, the bigger car and house, the better vacations, and more and more "stuff." In the long run, however, g-o-t-t-a doesn't spell fulfillment.

At each stage of life, the measurement of success differs. What a 20-year-old views as success may be radically different from the perspective of a 60-year-old. What doesn't change, however, is the fact that so many people don't do anything to get what they want. That you have reached this point— that you are reading this book—distinguishes you as someone who is willing to act. Success is extremely individual. You needed to do what you needed to do to get here. *Now make* *another choice —you don't have to go straight ahead.* There is nothing wrong with a "what's next?" attitude. It's how you apply it that matters:

TRAVEL LOG TIP:
For a couple of years following the release of the movie <u>Titanic</u>, my daughters had posters of Leonardo DiCaprio all over the walls of their rooms. I used to look at those posters and think what a great lesson the Titanic story gave us. As I explain to people in my seminars, when the Titanic crew saw the iceberg, they could not alter the course of the ship quickly enough. The "fastest" ship of all time was also the largest: It could not turn on a dime. But what could they have done if they had seen the iceberg 1,000 yards away, or 1 mile, 5 miles or 10 miles? At 1,000 yards, they would have had to turn the steering wheel a lot to miss the iceberg, and at 1 mile, only slightly. At 5 miles, the required turn of the wheel would have been less, and at 10 miles, only a slight turn of the wheel would have been needed to avert catastrophe. The point is that changing course isn't always about making a huge change; slight, incremental changes can be enough.   *Ken*

NOTES:

next possession, next status symbol, next debt? Or, next dream, next personal growth opportunity, next contribution to the world?

As we have said from the beginning, the choice is yours. Nothing happens by inaction. *Each thought,* *each idea creates the next and the next.* As long as movement occurs, your life plan remains dynamic. So allow yourself to daydream and let your imagination explore the possibilities. Don't let your ideas drift away. Grasp them and incorporate them into your plan. Keep a pad of paper and pen in strategic areas—in the car, by your bed, in the kitchen, next to your favorite chair— and jot them down.

As you move along toward your end-stage vision, your sense of possibility for yourself grows. As your sense of possibility for your-

TRAVEL LOG TIP:
Back in the 1970s, when I started consulting with long-term care facilities in California, I had to develop all the materials for each account by myself. It occurred to me one day that surely there must be other dietitians in Los Angeles who were consulting in long-term care, and I set out to find them. Within a few months, we had a group of about 20 nutrition professionals meeting to share ideas. Several of us thought we should start sharing materials with each other, rather than reinventing the wheel all the time. To my complete surprise, some members of the group were unwilling to share for fear that a fellow dietitian would steal an account from them. A small group of us did begin to share, however, and it paid us back richly. We were more successful, had more accounts and handled them more efficiently. There was strength in sharing. Now, some 30 years later, this group is a national organization and continues to be extremely successful.
Ellyn

NOTES:

self grows, you'll feel those old fears melting away—and as those fears disappear, you will eagerly explore new roads you never would have considered in the past. Point "Z" becomes not the end, but the beginning. Your journey is mapped not in one "A" to "Z" route, but in many interconnected routes. The future will never be as good as you imagine it—it will be better.

The Road Ahead

Getting to know yourself and discovering the depth and breadth of your potential not only opens a world of possibilities, it also opens your heart to others. Personal growth is accelerated through the absence of fear, and with that fear gone, it is easy to reach out to others.

It is difficult to describe the positive feeling that comes from helping someone overcome a challenge or solve a perplexing problem. Seeing growth in another person and knowing you had a hand in that growth creates a very special feeling of accomplishment. If you have ever helped a child take his or her first steps, you know the feeling. *It's as if a new world opens. There's no turning back—no more crawling through life.*

TRAVEL PLANNING
What's around the corner?

What goals have you accomplished in life?

___ Graduated from high school   ___ Married

___ Graduated from college   ___ Raised your children

___ Earned an advanced degree   ___ Joined a social club

___ Learned a craft

When you accomplished one of these goals, how did you determine what your next goal would be? _____

_____

_____

_____

Knowing what you know now, would you have seen more possibilities? _____

_____

Have you ever said, "If I had known then what I know now, I would have ___

_____ ."

How do you expect to feel when you accomplish your current goals? _____

_____

_____

_____

_____

With whom will you share your successes? _____

_____

As you achieve your goals, for whom can you be a role model? _____

_____

_____

R
O
A
D= DELIVER

11

Make Your Choices
Passenger, Driver ... or Navigator?

The corporate trainer is seated on his desk, legs dangling over the edge, as he waits for his "students" to come back for a final session. As he watches the men and women walk into the room, he observes how comfortable they have grown with each other.

Through the window, he eyes a few people still enjoying their last coffee break. The rest are now seated in the classroom and are engaged in pleasant conversation or bent over in fits of laughter. The "look" of this group of young leaders is certainly more comfortable than it was 14 days ago when the session started.

Here they are, gathered for the last session of "Young People with Potential." The trainer is supposed to offer some concluding remarks before the attendees are given their evaluations and dismissed.

Trainers know that most students forget 90 percent of what they hear 9 minutes after they hear it. Nevertheless, this trainer wants his final words to be special. He truly believes he has learned more from them than they have learned from him.

"I want to tell you a story," he begins, "about a day in my life that I had both anticipated and dreaded. It was the day that my eldest daughter was married. As a father, for me that day marked the last time I would hold her hand before placing it in the grasp of someone else.

"When she was born," he continues, "I welcomed her into my life, and now I was giving her away. All the years we had spent together, all the times I carried her so she wouldn't fall, the naps on my lap, the homework help, the dances and graduations—all of these memories were flooding into my mind. My wife and I totally accepted her husband-to-be, but all I knew was that everything was about change and would never again be the same.

"Any of you ever watch Steve Martin in *Father of the Bride*?" the trainer asks his students. There is a show of hands, and virtually everyone smiles at the reference.

"It's my daughter's favorite movie," the trainer says, "but let me tell you, it scared me more than *Jaws* or *The Exorcist* ever could. I feared the day that things would change. I've watched that movie several times, each time hoping that I would be able to draw some kind of strength or wisdom from it, but that never happened. Then the day finally arrived.

"Dads have this role at weddings," the trainer explains. "They're more 'keeper of the checkbook' than anything else. It's unfortunate in a way, because standing around in the midst of all that activity gives you more time to think—and to feel a little more sorry for yourself. I was headed down that path until something remarkable happened.

"Everything came down to that last minute," he says. "The guests were all seated, the bridesmaids had walked down the aisle and there in the vestibule stood two people—my daughter and me. I wanted to say something so special to her in that moment, something that would be perfect, but I was just speechless. Whatever words I had thought about previously had now completely escaped me. Then she looked at me through her veil, placed her hand in mine and said, 'Daddy, here next to me, that's right where you belong.' "

The trainer sees that his students are transfixed. Many are caught up in the story; some are lost in thought. All seem to understand the point he is trying to make.

"Right next to her was exactly where I belonged," he says. "We had spent 25 years together, and the years, tears, arguments, discussions and memories weren't coming to an end. All of those things had to happen so that this day could happen. Nothing was ending; it simply was being renewed, moving on to the next level."

"Ladies and gentlemen," the trainer says, "in a way that is what we are about today. We've gone through these sessions and shared a slice of life with one another. Now the time has come for this lesson in leadership to move to its next phase. I am where I belong and so are you.

"As we move into the future," he continues, "none of us knows where the road will take us. Some of you will be promoted, while others are relocated to another part of the country. Some of you may change jobs all together. No matter what lies ahead, though, we have had this time together to its good purpose.

"All of us are different than we were two weeks ago," he says. "Now it's my role to say good-bye to you and get ready to welcome the next class. It's your role to move on to your next challenge. Which of us has the more challenging role? Who's to say? But remember this: It's rarely what you do for yourself that really matters. Leadership is less about yourself and more about those you lead.

"Hold onto that thought throughout your career and your personal life," the trainer advises. "Your job as a leader is never to advance yourself but always to be willing to move those around you onward toward what awaits them. Do that and the feeling you are left with will be the greatest feeling possible. While it may not be the same as walking your daughter down the aisle, I can guarantee you that as a leader, you will be 'right where you belong.' "

~~~~~

Take a look at the cover of this book. Remember: We're challenging you to make a choice. On the road of life, are you a driver or a passenger? Are you willing to take charge of your life and move forward? Are you willing to be fueled less by fear and more by passion for your dream? Are you willing to dodge those potholes with a positive attitude? Are you willing to find your way around barricades and overcome your tendency to procrastinate? We hope you are nodding your head—yes, yes, yes and yes! *If so, step on the gas!* **GO**

TRAVEL LOG TIP:
When my children went off to college, I always wanted to be there for orientation so I could see all the clubs and organizations on campus. We would always discuss which ones they wanted to get involved with. As a parent, I felt it was my responsibility to encourage them to find their niche, learn, meet new people and grow from the experiences. As adults, we need to do the same thing: Get involved. Don't allow your fears to keep you from interacting with others. Working together in any capacity is a gift we give ourselves. I have never been involved in any organization in which I was not the major recipient of the giving. I have received friendship, knowledge and experience. To me, these are priceless.   *Ellyn*

NOTES:

Sharing the Ride

Once you are more secure in your own journey, you may be ready to slip into the passenger seat again—on someone else's journey. Feeling better about yourself and in control of your life will make it easy to give to others. This time, you won't be tagging along for the ride while someone else controls your decisions. Instead, you'll be taking the passenger seat as an active participant, helping someone else move from point "A" to point "B" and beyond.

When you've learned how to move forward in your own life, you will recognize that having control isn't a destination; it's a step—a big step, but still just a step. As you crest that hill with your life in gear and a full tank of positive attitude and passion, you can look into the future and see that life is not about control, but rather about sharing and supporting.

Chances are you will learn from those who support you in your journey that when two people have the same passion, tremendous creativity can result. Sharing a common belief and purpose generates energy that surpasses the capacity of one person alone. It is a classic case of the whole being greater than the sum of the parts. As you think back on your life, can you remember people who have been important to you? They are usually people who made you feel special, loved or significant. They are often people who stood for something and were steadfast in their commitments. You'll never forget those individuals. They added dimension to your life. *In whose life do you play that role?*

> TRAVEL LOG TIP:
> About 10 years ago, I drove to Denver with my daughter. Neither of us had ever seen a mountain before. When we reached the point where we could clearly see mountains ahead, we felt like we had arrived. We stopped to take in the extraordinary view. That lasted for about 10 minutes. Soon both of us were eager to expand our goal. It was no longer enough to "see" the mountains. Now we wanted to be "in" the mountains. So we fired up the engine and kept on moving forward. *Ken*
>
> NOTES:

All good investments mature over time. You'll experience this phenomenon as you make an investment in yourself. The more you put in, the more you'll get back. The same holds true for the investment you make in others. There comes a time when it's natural to begin focusing on others. As parents, teachers, mentors and bosses, we have the opportunity to touch the lives of others by providing direction and analyzing options—in other words, by navigating.

How you live your life and how you interact with others—how you share the ride—will be your legacy.

TRAVEL PLANNING
Will you make the trip alone?

Has anyone thanked you for helping him or her when you didn't even know you had? Who? Explain. _____

_____

_____

_____

_____

Have you thanked people who have helped you—even for just a small thing? Who? Give examples. _____

_____

_____

_____

_____

Do you realize when you have unintentionally influenced someone's life positively? Explain. _____

_____

_____

_____

_____

_____

Can you imagine the effect you could have with intentional support? Explain.

_____

_____

_____

_____

Have the Trip of Your Lifetime!

Put Yourself on the Map

The two grown brothers sit across from each other, avoiding direct eye contact. Both are searching their minds for the right words to use in this moment. Years before, fate had called them to separate and follow paths headed in opposite directions. Sadly, they had grown apart. It became difficult for them to relate to each other. The years passed with cordial conversations but never anything in depth. Soon they rarely talked at all.

Now, here they stand, scarcely three feet apart, and neither can find the words they need to say. The younger brother's mind is racing with thoughts of regret, loneliness and confusion. He feels a need to say, "You're the smart one here. Please, I need you. Tell me what I should do. Help me." But pride keeps the words at bay. He thinks, "Is all of this affecting you the way it is me?" But again, nothing is said aloud. Could these be the concerns of only one brother? Perhaps all the years and the miles have taken their final toll on the relationship. Perhaps there is just nothing left to say.

"Sorry for your loss," the funeral director says. "Will you two please guide the casket toward the altar?"

As they go through the motions of this ritual, their eyes meet. Instinctively, one smiles and the other winks. No words are needed.

The service lasts an hour as a parade of people find their way to the podium to extol a virtue or two. Even the clergyman is eloquent in his remembrances, even though he didn't really know the deceased man.

Each of the brothers, their spouses and the grandkids speak from their hearts and the memories seemed to bring everyone back together.

"He loved to go out on the lake, I remember how he taught me to put a worm on a hook."

"He pushed me for good grades. I wonder how I would have turned out if that hadn't happened."

"I am going to miss our talks."

"He sure lived for his grandkids."

"Thank you, God, for giving me this good man to be my husband all these years."

"Those flashcards, every night before dinner."

"He loved to listen to me, no matter what I had to say."

"Grandpa loved to play games, even dolls—he used to help me dress up the puppies."

"He told me he was proud of me. I'll never forget that."

"God, I could get mad at him but, oh, how I loved him!"

"Dad, you were my best friend."

"He was the best grandpa."

"Dad, I'm not going to forget anything, I promise."

"Grandpa, I want one more hug, one more look into your blue eyes."

"Thanks, Dad, I love you!"

"Grandpa, I'll miss you!"

"Grandpa, I love you!"

"We all love you!"

The service comes to an end as the casket is rolled out to the hearse. The small celebration of one man's life is over. But is it really? Would it ever really be over? The older son waits for the younger to walk beside him. He reaches out to grab an already outstretched hand. They know in this moment what the other is thinking: Despite their differences, they will always be brothers.

~~~~~

The legacy you deliver to the future is like a landmark. It's an historical marker commemorating your contribution to the world. Have you ever noticed that as soon as a map is drawn, it's usually out of date? Whether because of new roads or even new countries, maps are always improving with richness of information and detail. Isn't it time for your life to "be on the map?"

Destination You

When you think of the word "legacy," what comes to mind? Your rich uncle might leave you a financial legacy. You may take your money one day and give it to your alma mater for a new science lab, library or sports arena—the (your name here) building.

But there is another way to look at a legacy. For example, very few people alive today had the chance to hear the jazz of Ella Fitzgerald in person; to experience the tennis prowess and humanitarian work of Arthur Ashe; to see Audrey Hepburn on stage and witness her tireless work for the United Nations. Nevertheless, many of us have been influenced by the legacies of these people—the way they shaped our culture and the way they changed the world.

Although your legacy may not touch the lives of millions, you will be remembered. The question is how you will be remembered. After the money is spent and all the material things are gone, the most enduring and meaningful way to be remembered is in the lives of others. In Jewish tradition, one's 50th year is called the golden year. At age 50, you think about what you have accomplished and the lives you have touched. (When this tradition started, people didn't live much past age 50.) You don't have to be Jewish or 50 to do this exercise. The time is always right!

Living life like you mean it is living a life that brings you fulfillment, but you'll quickly learn that's only half of it. It's also touching the lives of others. Believing in yourself, creating your vision, pursuing your dreams—when you do this you become a person other people want to know more about, talk about and emulate. That's a legacy.

People aren't going to remember the car you drove, your clothes or your house, but they will remember the effect you had on them. When we

asked our friends and colleagues how they wanted
to be remembered, the
overwhelming answer was
"as a kind and giving person." If we are less than
we can be, it's because one
way or another, we chose
not to live up to our po-
tential. It comes down to
a question: *Are
you willing to
live with your-
self, knowing
that you are less
than you could be?*
Living like you mean it is
at its core an attitude—a
legacy mindset. Your leg-

TRAVEL LOG TIP:
My husband co-authored The Anatomy Coloring Book. It has sold more than 3 million copies. By taking a different approach to helping people learn the human anatomy, he has reached millions of students in the health professions and many others. He'll always be remembered for this. He went out on a limb. Many professors thought it was childish to use a coloring book to teach anatomy. But when the results were in, students who used his book scored higher marks than those who didn't.   *Ellyn*

NOTES:

acy will grow out of your attitude toward yourself, toward life and toward others.

No Idling, No Stalling

A noted author once wrote that a well-adjusted life is one that moves through three phases: dependence, independence and interdependence.[5] These phases are characterized by the nature of your relationships. A baby needs its parents to do everything, but as the child grows, he begins thinking and acting for himself. This independent activity is necessary for normal growth. Eventually, interdependence emerges as individuals accept their place in the lives of those around them.

We have all observed individuals who, regardless of age, have jumped off this evolutionary process at one phase or another and stayed there. We've all met fully grown adults who are still dependent on their parents or on society to provide for them. For many, the circumstances of life have made this experience unavoidable. But in many cases, these are people who never accept responsibility or are never allowed to think for themselves. Likewise, we've all observed fully grown, profoundly independent

Each of us has a story to tell, a story to leave for those who come after us. How we live our lives will be our story—our legacy. I find myself telling my children stories about their grandparents just as my parents told me stories about theirs. My parents are first-generation Americans. Our family came from Eastern Europe. My grandparents left a legacy now told through familiar stories and Yiddish expressions. I am so much of who I am because of them. And I want to be sure my memory of them stays alive through those whose lives I have a chance to touch.   *Ellyn*

NOTES:

people who operate without regard to the needs of others. For these people, life remains all about meeting their own needs.

And then there are those who see the importance of involving others in their lives and involving themselves in the lives of others. This is the evolution that is not only natural but also necessary for personal fulfillment.

Seeking a place of value in the lives of others is natural growth. We gather our families around us at life's most meaningful times. We mark our calendars and send out invitations. We draw our loved ones closer. These occasions are how life reminds us why we are here—to be present for one another and to have them be present for us in a healthy interdependence.

Blaze a New Trail

When you help others, you have more options and are more aware of opportunity. You are living a life with a legacy mind set. Imagine your ancestors as they decided to find a new life in a different country. In those times, families depended upon one another in a different way than they do now. The decision to pull up roots and move in a time when communication was slow and infrequent was profound. Imagine the discussions as dreams were shared and plans were made en route to a new life. Immigrants moved in with other immigrants as families worked together to start anew. Children grew up and moved out but often settled close by in an interdependent community. In one way or another, all of us are the result of legacy-producing decisions to pursue that dream of a new life.

At some point in life, everyone comes to the realization that having others in their lives is not only important but also essential. As people age, they may feel alone and vulnerable and wonder "what was my life worth?" Those who generously share their lives with others, give to others unselfishly and support others usually don't develop these feelings. They have a natural support system. Everyone has an opportunity to create this support. It's never too late to have the trip of your lifetime. It's never too late to put your legacy on the map. Start on the R.O.A.D. today: *Live like you mean it!*

TRAVEL LOG TIP:
I attended a seminar once with a group of about 150 managers. We were each given a deck of cards. Each card represented values such as "honesty" or "respect." The facilitator told us to separate the deck into two piles: things that are important to us and things that aren't as important. We were then instructed to pull our top 10 out of the "important" pile, then our top five, then our top two. Amazingly, 90 percent of the participants had either "faith," "family" or "legacy" among their most important choices.

Ken

NOTES:

TRAVEL PLANNING

Memories of a great trip

Can you identify some legacies left by your family members or friends? _____

_____

_____

_____

How do these legacies touch your life?_____

_____

_____

_____

Where are you in the process of moving from a dependent, to independent to interdependent life? _____

_____

_____

_____

Where would you like to be? How can you get there?_____

_____

_____

_____

If you were to die tomorrow, what would be your legacy? _____

_____

_____

_____

How would you like to be remembered? _____

_____

_____

Epilogue

Is That All There Is?

Ellyn: The answer to that question is yes—and no. Yes, reader, you're at the end of the book. And no, because as Ken and I hope you have realized, one of life's great gifts is that you can always have another dream, and another, and another ...

Ken: In fact the more dreams you have—the more often you hit the R.O.A.D.—the more new dreams will unfold along the way. The possibilities and opportunities are limited only by your imagination. We're not there yet, are we Ellyn?

Ellyn: Absolutely not! We're just getting started!

References

1. Kreigel RJ, Patler L. *If It Ain't Broke, Break It.* Warner Business Books; 1992.

2. *Report of the State of the American Bankruptcy System.* 1996 American Bankruptcy Institute. http://tinyurl.com/s3hce. Viewed May 3, 2006.

3. *The Quotable Walt Disney.* Disney Editions; 2001.

4. *BrainyQuote.* www.brainyquote.com/quotes/quotes/h/henry ford131621.html. Viewed May 3, 2006.

5. Covey SR. *The 7 Habits of Highly Effective People.* 15th ed. Free Press; 2004.

6. *The Quotable Walt Disney.* Disney Editions; 2001.

7. *BrainyQuote.* www.brainyquote.com/quotes/quotes/j/ johnfkenn121068.html. Viewed May 3, 2006.

8. *BrainyQuote.* www.brainyquote.com/quotes/quotes/b/benjamin fr109067.html. Viewed May 3, 2006.

9. Albom M. *The Five People You Meet in Heaven.* Hyperion; 2003.

10. Lundin SC, Paul H, Christensen J. *Fish! A Remarkable Way to Boost Morale and Improve Results.* Hyperion; 2000.

11. Barker JA. *Future Edge: Discovering the New Paradigms for Success.* William Morrow & Co.;1992.

12. *National Research Center for College and University Admissions.* www.nrccua.org/student/game.asp. Viewed May 3, 2006.

13. Mason K. College Students Change Career Paths As Often As They Change... Howard University. *The Hilltop.* March 31, 2006. www.tinyurl.com/o9ukn. Viewed May 3, 2006.